B Cohn
Cohn, Linda
Cohn-head : a
no-holds-barred account
of breaking into the boys
$24.95
ocn213838703
01/06/2009

More advance praise for *Cohn-Head*:

"Cohn-Head *is a candid, sweet, humorous, and intensely personal story of one of America's most recognized and well-liked sports media personalities. Linda Cohn is courageous enough to be introspective in a way that gives us insight into her personal evolution, from the difficulty of busting into the boy's club that is the sports television industry to battling through her inner conflicts to become a mother and role model.*"

**—Michael Wilbon, cohost of ESPN's *Pardon the
Interruption*, sports columnist for the *Washington Post***

"*Linda Cohn has been instrumental in the advancement of women in the media. Her wonderful book tells her story so well.*"

—Tim Kurkjian, ESPN's *Baseball Tonight* analyst

"*Linda Cohn grows up on Long Island yet becomes a Big New York Rangers fan, then goes to college at the snowiest place on earth where she excels as a goaltender. Out of college she gets into the man's world of TV sports and becomes a star. Who wouldn't want to read about this lady?*"

—Barry Melrose, head coach of the Tampa Bay Lightning

This book is dedicated to all of us who have found that the road to success is neither easy nor clear . . . and usually leads to somewhere other than where we expected it to go.

COHN-HEAD

A No-Holds-Barred Account of Breaking Into the Boys' Club

Linda Cohn

Foreword by Bill Walton

The Lyons Press

Guilford, Connecticut

An imprint of The Globe Pequot Press

The Lyons Press is an imprint of The Globe Pequot Press.

Photos by the author unless otherwise noted
Text design by Sheryl Kober

Library of Congress Cataloging-in-Publication Data

Cohn, Linda.
Cohn-head : a no-holds-barred account of breaking into the boys' club / Linda Cohn.
p. cm.
Includes index.
ISBN 978-1-59921-113-8
1. Cohn, Linda. 2. Sportscasters--United States--Biography. 3. Women broadcast-
ers--United States--Biography. I. Title.
GV742.42.C63A2 2008
070.4'49796092--dc22
[B]
2008012806

Printed in the United States of America
10 9 8 7 6 5 4 3 2 1

Contents

Truth

One of the first lessons I learned in journalism was to be genuine. That was a good thing, because I am a terrible liar. All of the
events in this book are true and accurate to the best of my recol-
lection. I have not gone through life recording every conversation I ever had. As a result, any dialogue quoted in this book is
the way I remember it. Throughout this book, I have changed
names, places, and incidental events not pertinent to the story
in order to protect the innocent and, in some cases, the guilty.

Acknowledgments

Special thanks go to Rob Kirkpatrick, senior editor at The Lyons Press, who gently guided me and allowed me the freedom to write the book I wanted to write. Also, to Tom McCarthy, executive editor, who pulled these pages out of their free-fall and turned them into the book you hold in your hand today.

My parents, for better and worse, set the foundation for the person I am today. Mom, I know, wherever you are—probably at the Great Tennis Club in the Sky—you are handing out copies of this book to everyone you know. Hank, you gave me my passion for sports, which has made all the difference.

To my siblings—Ilene, Howie, and Donna—I probably never would have survived my childhood without you guys. I love you.

I have worked very hard to get to this point in my career, but it might have taken a completely different path if it were not for some very special people: Frank Brinka, Mike Farrell, Ted David, Peter Goldberg, Ed Ingles, John Lippman, Fritz Messere, Lea Tyrell, Shelby Whitfield, and Shelly from Seattle.

It would be inexcusable of me not to acknowledge every one of my ESPN colleagues, past and present. They have provided my home away from home for fifteen years. I must single out, though, those who either helped me refresh my faulty memory for this book or were always there when I needed them: John Anderson, Chris Berman, Steve Berthiaume, Jud Burch, Rich Eisen, Neil Everett, Brian Kenny, Keith Olbermann, Gus Ramsey, Stuart Scott, Lya Vallat, Elida Witthoeft, and Norby Williamson.

Acknowledgments

Even among all these special people, Steve Anderson deserves a special mention for his selfless counsel.

Also, a special and sincere thank you to Al Jaffe. Al is the guy at ESPN who negotiates all of the contracts. He is *very* good at his job, but also fair and open. Thanks Al.

To Bob Costas, thanks for your wisdom. Who knows? You may have saved my life.

Looking back, it is hard for me to believe that, at one time, I didn't think I wanted to have children. In a life filled with thrills, Sammy and Daniel are my shining stars and more important to me than anything else in this world.

Any attempt at acknowledging what Stew has done for me will fall short. The absolute, very least I can say is that, without him, this book would never have been written.

Foreword

I'm a Cohn-Head Too

Wow! Linda Cohn's fascinating new narrative of life and love in the testosterone-driven world of American sports and ESPN is an excellent tale of one dynamic woman's charging crusade to have it her way. While it seems that the 149 miles from Linda's hometown of Coram, Long Island, to ESPN's campus in Bristol, Connecticut, is but a hop, skip, and jump, the reality of this most unlikely journey is what mandates our interest in *Cohn-Head*. As with most trendsetting artists who seem to be generations ahead of their time, Linda's ultimate success and acceptance has not come easy. But it is her unique ability to paint a multi-hued canvas of alternating hope and devastation in this riveting saga, much the way she captures our imagination and soul on a nightly basis on ESPN, that drives our clamoring and insatiable desire for more of Linda Cohn.

Cohn-Head bares it all both personally and professionally: from battles won and lost, to dreams realized and shattered; from grandiose plans, to demoralizing suppression. Linda is the master storyteller unchained by the relentless time clock at ESPN. And it is in her tantalizing anecdotes, brilliantly organized and passionately recounted, that we come to understand our own commitment and loyalty to this true American icon. We choose to invite Linda Cohn into our homes and life every time we tune in to ESPN. Her creativity, honesty, wit, imagination, accuracy, talent, durability, beauty, and grace bring us back for more everyday, because we know what we're going to get from Linda—her unpredictable best. But at ESPN, it's all but a tease, where she's constantly covered by highlights, draped by statistics, anchored to the *SportsCenter* desk, and always cut short by the race to get to that next commercial appeal for you to buy something.

Reading *Cohn-Head* was more than I could ever hope for: all Linda, all the time. No commercials, no products, no producers, no limits and—like all things Linda Cohn—no nonsense. The love affair that America has with Linda is based on trust, faith, integrity, class, dignity, and her unlimited lust for joyous fun. *Cohn-Head* is the uncensored and boundless masterpiece that validates our loyalty to this true genius and angel of mercy. And Linda reluctantly points out what we already know: She is simply "just too sexy." And this is just one of the many reasons why our infatuation and love for her will never fade away. As with all things Linda Cohn, we can't wait for what's next, and *Cohn-Head* is our time-traveling spaceship with Linda at the controls. What more could anybody ask for?

Hold on everybody—and enjoy the ride!

—Bill Walton

ONE

How I Became a
Stark Raving Mad Sports Fan

Before we get started talking about how I grew up to become Linda Cohn, sportscaster extraordinaire, you should know that when I was a freshman in college, I came home for Thanksgiving and destroyed every old picture of me I could find. I don't want to say my life before college sucked. Or that I spent most of my adolescence alone in my room, listening to sad songs on a little nine-volt transistor radio and feeling sorry for myself. So let me just put it another way: When I came home for that first Thanksgiving after going away to college, I definitely was not going to my high school Homecoming Dance to reminisce with old friends. And the Saturday after that Thanksgiving, when I was in the Smith Haven Mall and saw Jessie from my senior-year bookkeeping class walking toward me, I turned around and ran away. That's right, I ran away, because I just didn't want anything to do with that part of my life, and I didn't want to spend any time talking to someone who was probably wondering if my existence was any less pathetic in college than it had been in high school.

To be honest, I don't really remember a lot of the details from my "formative years." It's probably post-traumatic shock syndrome or something like that. You know what I mean: I've subconsciously suppressed all of those bad memories so I can live a relatively normal life. Maybe not the healthiest approach, but it seems to have worked for me. The only problem is, now that I'm writing this book I've had to dredge up all those old memories. Luckily, looking back through the veil of time, it all seems kind of funny and not quite as pitiful as it did back then.

If you were to see a snapshot of my life growing up, you might think I had a *Brady Bunch* type of childhood, a typical, antiseptic, white middle-class upbringing. In reality, my upbringing was a little more twisted. To start with, my parents' names were the same as the Munsters'—Herman and Lillian—not the Bradys'. Okay, the mother in *The Munsters* was really named Lilly, but close enough.

Like I said, on the outside things looked pretty normal. I lived in a raised ranch, in Coram, Long Island, with Herman and Lillian, my two sisters, my brother, and our dog Ginger. Ginger was a beautiful, tricolor collie I had picked out because I thought she was the most beautiful dog in the world. To everyone in my family, including me, beauty was the most important thing. In our house, the saying "Beauty is only skin deep" was not only never uttered, it was completely incomprehensible.

Another basic truth in our household was that we were all proclaimed by Herman and Lillian as the best at whatever we did. My mother was the best nurse in the world, even though she happened to work at Macy's—yes, the department store—and spent most of her time administering aspirin and Band-Aids to customers with headaches and paper cuts. My dad managed to be the best accountant in the world, even though he hated his job and spent his entire career wishing he had become a journalist, a merchant marine, or just about anything but an accountant. My siblings had their own qualities at which they were considered the best, but, more importantly, I was deemed by my parents, and especially my father, to be "the most beautiful girl in the world." Never mind how my two sisters felt about this when my father would praise my beauty in front of them. In a home where beauty was anything but skin deep, being the most beautiful girl in the world made me the best, and I was all about me.

As you may have guessed—remember, I destroyed all my childhood pictures—I had some difficulty reconciling my title as "most beautiful girl in the world" with what I saw in the mirror, and this contradiction proved to have some long-lasting effects on me. Here's a short list: It made me distrustful of praise in general; it negated any legitimate praise I received from my parents; it made me feel like a phony (because I knew I wasn't really the most beautiful girl in the world), it made me feel full of entitlement (because I still wanted to *believe* I was the most beautiful girl in the world and that I deserved everything that came with that title), it made me resentful, it made me sad, and it made me feel inferior. Well, that's what I've figured out so far anyway. Give me another twenty years and I might be able to add to the list.

To set the record straight, I wasn't one of those stunningly attractive girls who walked the halls of my school complaining that I was ugly so my equally beautiful girlfriends would quickly run to my defense and tell me how beautiful I really was.

No. I think I had a pretty good handle on where I landed on the list of most beautiful girls in school, and it was pretty close to the bottom. I was skinny (not attractively thin, but gangly and bony with elbows and knees sticking out everywhere), and I had long, dark, completely unmanageable curly hair that accentuated my pale, freckly face; and those were my good points. The worst thing about how I looked was that I had unbearably thick tortoiseshell glasses.

My vision was about 20/300. That meant my glasses were almost half an inch thick and they made my green eyes—the only physical attribute I liked about myself—look like little dark, piercing beads. On top of that, wearing glasses that thick was kind of like wearing horse blinders, because I could only see what was directly in front of me. Even if I'd felt confident enough to believe that other kids would be interested in talking with me, I couldn't really see them unless they were right in front of me. Of course, that wasn't really a problem, because I didn't want anyone to notice me and my big fat glasses anyway. I just wanted to fade into the background and be left alone.

Back at home, I pretty much kept to myself too. Coming home from school, I would usually just go to my room, make a halfhearted attempt at my homework, and then listen to DJs like Ron Lundy and Cousin Brucie on WABC-AM radio. I loved all the pop music of the 1960s and '70s—"Sugar Sugar" by the Archies, "Sweet Caroline" by Neil Diamond, and anything by the Beatles—but my favorite songs were always the sad and heart-wrenching ones they played late at night. One of my all-time favorites was "I Started a Joke" by the Bee Gees in which, Robin Gibb—who, like me, wasn't the most attractive person you ever saw—sang about making the world a better place by dying.

Was I pathetic or what? Another reason I stayed in my room a lot was because my mother was an emotional roller coaster and probably should have been on medication. Seriously, looking back, I think my mother may have been schizophrenic. At any given moment, I never knew until it was too late which mom I was dealing with. About half the time I would run into the loving, caring, selfless mom whose total support and belief would be a major factor in my later professional success. The other half I encountered a screaming, maniacal, crazy lady who could find fault in anything and everything. Honestly, the littlest thing could set her off: my dad's driving, my sister's wedding, a board game, even the Beatles.

Don't believe me? Let me tell you how the Beatles drove her past the brink of insanity. It was on a day when my mother was working late at Macy's. No one else was in the house, and I was in the living room, where we had a new eight-track stereo. I was listening to the Beatles' *Sgt. Pepper's Lonely Hearts Club Band* album. "A Day in the Life," the last song on the album, was playing.

To set the scene, let me remind you that this song alternates eerie, dreamlike segments sung by John Lennon with an upbeat, pop-oriented middle segment sung by Paul McCartney. At the end of each dreamlike sequence, there's this big orchestral cacophony that sounds like every instrument in the orchestra is playing faster and higher until it ends in a big crescendo. At the time, there was a rumor that Paul had died in a car accident and had been secretly replaced by a look-alike. "A Day in the Life" was supposed to contain secret clues about what had happened to Paul. I bought into the whole thing.

Paul was the "cute" Beatle and, as you might expect, my favorite. So I was especially intent on listening to the words of "A Day in the Life" and trying to decode its secret meaning whenever I heard it. As usual, I was lying on the floor with my head close to the speakers and my eyes closed. I was in my own little world, being carried away by the music, and I didn't hear my mother come into the house through the garage. I wouldn't have cared anyway, because I was immersed in the rising sounds of that second crescendo, thinking about Paul.

My mother, in comparison, was not so moved by the song's intensity. Nor was she apparently concerned whether or not Paul was dead. I'm not exactly sure what happened when she came into the house that day. All I know is that just as the crescendo was about to peak, the music stopped with a shudder and I heard the eight-track tape being yanked out of its player. I opened my eyes, not knowing what I was going to see, and there was my mother bent over me, her face full of rage and her eyes bulging out, screaming something at me that I couldn't possibly understand. Then she smashed the tape on the floor, stomped on it a few times, and walked downstairs to do some laundry, leaving me to clean up the mess she had made. She never mentioned it again.

That's usually how it happened. Without any warning, my mother would go ballistic, scream at the top of her lungs, smash something, and walk away to do the laundry. Sometimes, if she was angry and none of us was near enough for her to yell at, she would smash something just to get our attention. Then, when we came running, she would scream at us for some horrible injustice that we had supposedly rendered upon her. Usually, though, she was unhappy about something that had nothing to do with us and was just transferring her anger about that unhappiness onto us.

She was one of those people who found lots of things to be unhappy about, but most of the time she was unhappy with the way she looked. My mother was not a thin woman. On top of that, the styles being what they were in the '70s, she spent most of her work day wearing a tight, white nurse's uniform that accentuated her size. Since she, like all of the Cohn clan, equated attractiveness with value, she was often unhappy with herself.

Growing up with a mother like this, I learned to associate any sudden, loud noise with impending doom. I also learned that if you felt bad about something, the best way to feel better was to blame how you felt on someone else. If you think that's good, wait until I tell you about the Talking Couch where my mother, wrought with her own problems, tried to resolve the trials and tribulations of her offspring . . . but that's later. For now, let's talk about sports!

The first sport I learned to play was tennis. It was also the first thing I ever remember being good at. It was 1972, and there was that whole tennis craze going on with John McEnroe, Jimmy Connors, Chris Evert, and Billie Jean King. My mother had started taking tennis lessons, and she developed a real passion for it. Since I was the only one in the family who showed any interest in what she was doing, she signed me up for lessons too.

I was still wearing glasses, but it didn't bother me on the tennis court because Billie Jean King, who had already won Wimbledon, the French Open, and the US Open, wore glasses too. She was my first sports idol. I liked her because, by my reckoning, she wasn't any better looking than I was and she just didn't seem to care. Even though Chris Evert—who was blond and beautiful—got all the media attention, Billie Jean kicked butt on the court and won equal respect and admiration for her abilities. I saw that people liked her despite her looks. That was a new concept for me, and I kind of liked it. I also liked that, the following year, Billie Jean stood up to Bobby Riggs, a fifty-five-year-old former tennis great who boasted that he could beat any female tennis player in the world. He was a trash talker before they knew what trash talkers were, and he liked to exclaim that women were just inferior to men. Billie Jean killed him in three sets: 6–4, 6–3, 6–3. I think that was when I first started to realize that a woman was capable of anything.

After I'd taken tennis lessons for a while, it turned out that I had some natural skill on the court and I actually liked playing. I also liked the attention I got when I won—and so I always played to win. Dave, my tennis instructor, told my mother he thought I could make a name for myself if I stuck with it. A bright spot in my future, that was something new.

Once I discovered tennis, I became interested in other sports, starting with basketball and the Knicks. In our home, on any typical evening, my siblings and I would go to our rooms after dinner to do whatever, and my mother would head off to do the laundry—now that I think about it, I guess we had a lot of laundry. My dad, whom we all called Hank, would go downstairs to try to stay out of my mother's way and watch whatever sporting event was on TV. In the late fall and winter, during the week, that meant the Knicks.

When people meet Hank, they usually find him instantly likable. He is warm, almost never gets angry, is quick with a compliment, and loves to laugh. He isn't, and never was, what you would call fatherly, however, and, although he loved my mother, he spent much of his time either working or, like me and my siblings, trying not to set my mother off. His way of escaping was to sit in front of the TV downstairs and watch sports. In a lot of ways, he was more like an older brother than a father. Maybe that's why we called him Hank instead of Dad.

To get closer to Hank, I started wandering downstairs to watch the Knicks with him and found out I liked basketball almost as much as I liked tennis. There wasn't much tennis to watch in the winter and, certainly, compared with my nonexistent social life, basketball was exciting and full of emotion. I loved the fast pace and thrill of competition, and there was something special about watching a team sport that was exhilarating and different from tennis. When the Knicks won, I was euphoric. When they lost I was sad, but that was still better than the bland nothingness of my everyday existence.

My favorite player on the Knicks was Walt Frazier. He was the team captain, got a lot of attention, and had a cool nickname: Clyde. That whole season, Hank and I sat in front of the TV, screaming, crying, and yelling, but mostly cheering as we watched the Knicks win the championship. I watched Clyde's every move; Hank cheered on his own favorite, Willis Reed. Before most games, Hank would stop at the bakery and bring home a linzer torte for me to have during the game. It was a great time for me and my dad, and linzer tortes have been my favorite bakery dessert ever since.

I liked basketball so much that I played on the junior varsity team that winter. Unfortunately, while I was a natural on the tennis court, I wasn't much of a basketball player, so I quit at the end of the season. If I couldn't be really good at basketball, I didn't want to play. Hey, I'm not saying I'm proud of that thinking, but that's how I was.

After they won the championship that year, Walt Frazier, Willis Reed, and Dave DeBusschere made an appearance at the Smith Haven Mall, near where I lived. Times were different then, and appearing at the mall was considered a good gig for a trio of basketball greats. As soon as we found out they would be there, Hank and I made our plans to go. Each player was making his appearance in a different section of the mall, so when we got there Hank headed over to see Willis Reed and I ran off to see Walt Frazier.

I can't even begin to tell you how excited I was. I had lived and died with the Knicks that season. Their wins were my own personal victories, and their losses were my own defeats. Of course, we did win the championship, so it was all good in the end. The only thing that could have been more exciting to me than seeing Walt Frazier would have been meeting David Cassidy, the man of my dreams—and those of every other thirteen-year-old girl in my school—who played Keith Partridge on *The Partridge Family*. In other words, seeing Walt Frazier was big!

We had gotten to the mall early, so there was really no one else at the stage when I got there. I parked myself right in front. After a while the crowd began to build—and so did my anticipation. I had pretty close to an ideal spot by the stage and I was just about the only girl in the crowd, so every now and then someone would see an opportunity and try to nudge me out of the way. I didn't care. I held my own. I wasn't going to let anyone get between me and Walt Frazier, even if I had to give them a push or an elbow to keep my place, which I did, more than once.

Finally, after what seemed like forever, Walt Frazier walked onto the stage to a roaring ovation. He moved to the center of the stage right in front of me and looked around at the crowd going wild. Even though he was a big star, he actually seemed moved by the crowd's appreciation. Then he turned his head downward in my direction. He bent down and, looking right at me, whispered, "Wow." Even today, I don't know if he really saw me there or if it just seemed that way to a starstruck thirteen-year-old. It didn't matter. All I knew was that I had shared a personal moment with Walt Frazier—and that one day I too wanted to be able to stand in front of a crowd of adoring fans, kneel down to a kid in the front row who knew what I was talking about, and whisper "Wow."

In the spring of that year, I also discovered Mets baseball. Hank had always been a Yankees fan, but I had recently become friends with Patricia, a girl in my school who collected baseball cards and was a crazy Mets fan, so I became one too. Yes, as hard as it may be to believe, I was starting to make friends. I was also friends with Joan, who was a big Beatles fan like me, and we used to walk around acting silly and speaking in British accents. I wasn't exactly a social butterfly, but I was moving in the right direction.

That summer my family joined the Stonybrook Swim and Tennis Club. (We called it "The Club" because it made it sound fancier.) What I remember about The Club was that they had two pools, there was a great snack bar, and *everybody* played tennis. I had been playing tennis for two years now and I was getting pretty good. I was so good, in fact, that I was ranked third among all the women at The Club and I had all these thirty-something guys lining up to ask me to be in their mixed-doubles competitions.

What a thrill! I was just a pale fourteen-year-old girl with glasses who didn't get even a casual look from the boys at my school, but at The Club I had tanned, thirty-year-old men in white shorts asking me if I would please play doubles with them. In between matches I would lie in the sun with my other new friend, Beth, from The Club listening to Bob Murphy announce the Mets games. The Mets were having a horrible season, but at least I had three friends now!

The following winter I discovered something I loved more than tennis or basketball or baseball or even David Cassidy—hockey! Hank had always been a big Rangers fan, but it was the second year of the New York Islanders franchise, and they were getting a lot of publicity. Sports coverage wasn't as wide back then and there were very few TV broadcasts of the fledgling Islanders, so I started listening to their games on the radio in my room.

I can't really articulate what it is about hockey that was, and is, so exciting to me. If you're a hockey fan, then you already know. If you're not, all I can say is that it has something to do with the unbelievably fast pace of a game played on ice, the physical interaction of the players, and knowing that at any time a goal can be scored that will completely change the direction and pace of the game.

On one of the walls in my room, I created a collage of goalie pictures I cut from sports and hockey magazines. I was drawn to goalies from the start because they were always the center of attention. I just thought, sure, goalies had so much pressure, but they could also be the hero of the game and, by the way, did I mention that they were the center of attention? When the goalie made a great save, the other players would come up to him and pat him on his pads with their sticks; and when the goalie let in a tough shot, his teammates would come by and pat him on his pads anyway to let him know it was okay; and if the team won, it was the goalie who got all the love! That's what I wanted, all the love.

The only problem was that back in the day, girls weren't allowed to play ice hockey, so I did what a lot of girls who wanted to play ice hockey did those days: I joined the girls' field hockey team. As it turned out, field hockey and I didn't get along too well. I, of course, wanted to be the goalie, but having never played or even watched a field hockey game before, I didn't realize that the role of a goalie on a field hockey team was much different from that of a goalie on an ice hockey team. Whereas nearly all of the action in an ice hockey game occurs near the net, in a field hockey game very little of it does. I became goalie so I would be the center of attention. Instead, and just like the rest of my life, as the goalie I was often forgotten. On top of that, standing in the goal in the late fall wearing one of those short, plaid skirts could get kind of drafty.

Despite the drafts and the lack of attention, I was the team's only goalie and I knew I had a responsibility to show up to every game and play my best. That's what team sports were all about for me. Then in October, Yom Kippur, the holiest day on the

Jewish calendar, landed on the same day as a game. My mother was adamant. There was no way she was going to let me play field hockey on the "Day of Judgment."

Just a quick aside, as most Jews know, in 1965 Sandy Koufax, the left-handed pitcher for the Los Angeles Dodgers, famously decided not to pitch in the first game of the World Series against the Minnesota Twins because it was Yom Kippur. Instead, he fasted (as is the tradition), and went to temple to pray.

Though I knew the story of Sandy Koufax and thought of myself as a good Jew, I didn't see how that story applied to me. I was my team's only goalie, and they were depending on me. I wasn't going to miss that game. Under almost any other circumstances, I wouldn't even have thought about mixing it up with my mother. I could get in enough trouble just by listening to the Beatles; I definitely didn't want to invite her into an argument. But this was different. I had a responsibility to my team, and I wasn't going to let them down. So we argued and screamed at each other until my mother finally backed down and agreed to take me to the game.

On the way to the game, my mother was stopped by a police car for speeding. To her, that was the sign from God she was expecting. She fully believed that God had given her a speeding ticket because she was driving her daughter to a field hockey game on Yom Kippur. As for me, I thought she got the ticket because she was doing 40 miles an hour in a 30 mph zone. Call me crazy. Despite the ominous sign from God, we continued on our way to the game, and we won.

Meanwhile, back in the NHL, the Islanders had a dismal season and didn't even make the playoffs. If you're a hockey fan, you know the playoffs last about two and a half months, so if your team doesn't make it, you miss out on three months of the most exciting hockey of the season. If you're fourteen years old, that means you have to find another favorite team. I defected to Hank's team, the Rangers, and never looked back. Hey, give me a break, I was fourteen. I was allowed to change my mind.

Although I've never regretted my defection to the Rangers, I was punished by sports karma that next season. This was my second year following hockey, and I expected the upcoming season to be pretty much like the previous: The Islanders would place last in the East, like they had in the previous season, and my newly beloved Rangers would be contenders for the Stanley Cup.

The difference was, this season we expected the Rangers to win the Stanley Cup. In 1975 the Rangers were considered, at least by New Yorkers, a team of superstars. They had such greats as Rod Gilbert, Phil Esposito, Pete Stemkowski, Ron Greschner, and my latest idol, goalie Eddie Giacomin. I thought Eddie Giacomin was unbelievable. Unlike the other Rangers' goalie, Gilles Villemure, who was often criticized, at least by fifteen-year-old me, for just standing there waiting for the puck to whiz by him, Eddie was aggressive and gutsy. He was always coming out of the net to assist his defensemen and he would drop down to the ice for a save and pop right back up, ready for the next shot on goal. When I started playing ice hockey myself a few years later, I modeled my style after Eddie, and it was his number I wore: #1. That was perfect, because I was a simple girl. All I wanted was to be #1. Was that too much to ask?

In comparison with the Rangers, the Islanders weren't considered a threat to anyone. The previous season, Islanders GM Bill Torrey drafted top pick defenseman Denis Potvin and convinced St. Louis Blues coach Al Arbour to come to Long Island, but the team still wasn't able to move up the ranks.

In 1975, though, things began to gel for the Islanders and they earned their first playoff berth. I was very happy, but not for the Islanders. I was completely done with the Islanders, but I was happy that they were going to be playing the Rangers in the first round of the playoffs. It was a best-of-three series, and everyone thought the Rangers were going to sweep the Islanders, a team that had never even been in the playoffs before.

Well, we were all in for a rude awakening. In the first game, at the Rangers' Madison Square Garden, the Islanders won. After two games the Rangers and Islanders were tied at one game apiece. The third and deciding game was on a Saturday night back at Madison Square Garden. I was babysitting the Wilson boys down the street. The boys were asleep and I was downstairs, watching the game, alone, in the dark. To my shock, Eddie Giacomin was not in the goal. Instead they had put Gilles Villemure in the net, and he proceeded to allow three goals to pass by him in the first period. They weren't even good goals. All of them were 40 feet out and at bad angles. I was screaming at the TV to get Villemure out of there. I knew I should be careful not to wake the Wilson boys up, but this was hockey. I was out of control.

To their credit, the Islanders had no fear. They played like they were on fire and celebrated every goal like they were playing in front of a home crowd. With the Rangers utterly demoralized, they finally brought Eddie Giacomin into the goal. Eddie had a big job ahead of him, but he knew what he had to do. He started a fight with Garry Howatt, the toughest guy on the Islanders team.

Now, don't get all excited. I hate fighting in the NHL. I think it takes away from the game, attracts the wrong element, and can be life threatening. I applaud the tougher stance the league has taken over the last few years. I think it has improved the game. That said, I think there are occasional situations in every sport that warrant a measured act of aggression.

This was one of those times. Eddie's fight turned the momentum of the game around, and the third period ended with the Rangers and Islanders tied 3–3. Sitting in the dark in front of the TV, I could tell the Rangers were going to pull through in overtime. Alas, it was not meant to be. As the ref dropped the puck at center ice, it made its way into the Rangers' corner. Steve Vickers was right there battling with a couple of Islanders to gain control of the puck, although it didn't look to me like he was trying that hard. Then one of the Islanders managed to kick it out in front of the net and right over to the Islanders' J. P. Parise, who knocked it in the net only eleven seconds into overtime, a record at the time. I called Hank, who was watching the game at home, and we commiserated on the phone for over an hour until we both felt better enough to go on with our lives.

That was the first game where I really got it. I understood what a sporting event could do to you, and I began to see what it was going to be like as a Rangers fan. In just one game, the Rangers had taken me so low that I was screaming at the TV and about to cry, raised me so high that I was in a euphoric frenzy, and then, eleven seconds into overtime, threw me with a thud into what felt like a manic depression.

For the Islanders, it was a defining win. They went on to the semifinals and took the Flyers to a final game before losing, just as the Rangers had done the year before. After that, a lot of Rangers fans who were tired of what they thought of as a fat-cat mentality switched over to the Islanders, but not me. Although I had made a slight detour, I knew I had been born to be a Rangers fan, for better or worse—and for me the rivalry between the Rangers and Islanders had become personal.

Back in the real world my life completely changed one day when my mother took me to the eye doctor to get contact lenses. I was still pale, skinny, and freckly, but at least now I had a face that people could see. It was also life altering because it showed me in a way I had never seen before that my parents really cared about me a lot. You see, for reasons too complicated to explain here, we lived in a kind of middle-class poverty. Sure, we had a nice enough house in the suburbs and belonged to The Club where we played tennis all summer, but we also always seemed to be short on money. For instance, while we were one of the first families on our block to have a built-in dishwasher, we had to wash our dishes by hand because we didn't have the money to repair it after it broke. The same was true with our air-conditioning. We had central air-conditioning but lived for more than five years without using it because we couldn't afford to replace the broken compressor.

Another thing that happened about the same time I got contacts was that I discovered some neighborhood boys around the corner—including David Simon, who is now a researcher at ESPN—playing street hockey. No one in their group really wanted to play goalie; so even though these boys were five years younger than me, they accepted my offer to defend the net for them. I didn't care about the age difference, I just wanted to play hockey. With some old baseball equipment and a standard hockey stick, I started developing my goalie skills by blocking tennis balls flung at me by fifth graders.

When *I* was in fifth grade, I wanted to learn to play the drums, but my mother wouldn't let me. She thought playing the drums wasn't very feminine and she made me take the violin instead. Now I was this teenage girl playing street hockey with fifth graders. Not only wasn't that very feminine, it was actually pretty weird.

Soon after I started playing street hockey with the boys around the corner, my mother told me she had read about a recreational hockey league at the Racquet and Rink in Farmingdale that let girls play. That's right: The very same mother who wouldn't let me play the drums because they were too masculine was encouraging me to play ice hockey. On top of that, she said she was willing to make the ninety-minute round trip drive with me three times a week so that I could practice with the team and play in the games.

I remember going to get my first set of skates and goalie equipment. I was so excited I couldn't stand it. Of course, times were different then, and I got a lot of strange looks from the salesmen and other customers as I was trying on pads and goalie masks. None of them had ever heard of a girl playing hockey, but I didn't care. My mother believed in me and told me I could succeed in anything if I put my mind to it, and I believed it too.

The only obstacle to my becoming a goalie with the skills of Eddie Giacomin was that I couldn't skate. Sure, I had gone ice-skating a few times with my family, but I was one of those kids who always stayed close to the rail and kind of wobbled forward uneasily with my arms spread out for balance. I don't think I ever made it all the way around the rink without falling at least once.

I'm not sure why I wasn't concerned about not being able to skate, but I wasn't. Maybe it was because my mother never seemed to be concerned about doing things she wasn't qualified for. I know I've made fun of my mother being a nurse at Macy's, but that's not what I'm talking about. My mother really was a good nurse, and she was dedicated to her job. She was always organizing blood drives and bringing in health professionals to speak to employees about the latest health issues. In other areas, however, she was a little less qualified and, perhaps, not very realistic.

Like I said, despite both my mother and father being professionals, we always seemed to be scraping around for cash. In response, my mother was always looking for some way to strike it rich. One of the ways she tried to do this was by selling weight loss programs door-to-door. I think the first one she tried was called Cambridge Systems, but over the years she tried her hand at about half a dozen programs.

I hope, at this point, you're beginning to understand that, despite her faults, I loved my mother very much and we always had a close, if tumultuous, relationship. That said, there's no denying my mother did not even slightly resemble the "after" pictures in the weight loss brochures she gave out to prospective customers. Although she never discussed her successes or failures, looking back, I think it's fair to say, given the way she was always switching to a new or better weight loss company, that she wasn't a top earner. Even so, she never gave up. I guess some people would look at this and say my mother was just delusional. What I saw was a mother who truly believed she could do anything she put her mind to and didn't give up.

With a role model like that, it was natural for me to think I could start playing ice hockey without being able to skate. My first day at the rink, I was a little nervous and excited because it was my first time playing ice hockey, but I barely gave a thought to the fact that I couldn't skate. I just stepped out on the ice.

Maybe it was the stability provided by my forty pounds of goalie equipment, or maybe it was just because I was determined to succeed. Whatever the reason, I was able to step out on the ice, go through the drills, and drop down for saves almost right away. I found it was definitely easier to drop down and pop back up on the ice than it was when I was playing street hockey.

Of course, I wasn't what you would call a good skater, but I was good enough to start out. Over the next few weeks of practice, I learned to turn, skate backward, and generally remain upright. Even though none of my teammates knew it, I was a much better skater with my equipment on than without it because that's how I had learned to skate. I don't think they would have cared much anyway. You see, when I played street hockey I was playing with ten-year-olds, but in the ice hockey league they started me out with eight-year-olds.

What a sight I must have been to the parents who came out to watch their little boys play ice hockey for the first time. I was still fighting extreme shyness and low self-esteem, but I stood a good 6 to 8 inches taller than any of my teammates, and in bulky goalie equipment with a ponytail sticking out the back of my red, white, and blue star-spangled goalie mask, I definitely stood out. Maybe it was because I was able to hide behind the mask, but I wasn't self-conscious at all. I actually thought I was very cool and I always got a big reaction from the crowd, which I loved. A good part of that reaction was probably shock at seeing a fourteen-year-old girl playing goal for a bunch of eight-year-old boys, but I always interpreted it as people thinking, *A girl in goal. How cool!*

I kept playing ice hockey at the Racquet and Rink all through junior high and high school, and I was getting better and better, although I was still playing with boys at least four years younger than me. I longed to play with people my own age. At the end of my sophomore year and the beginning of my junior year, while other girls were planning their sweet sixteen parties, I was trying to decide exactly how crazy I would have to be to try out for the boys' high school ice hockey team.

Even though I had been playing ice hockey now for about three years, I was a wreck. I wasn't nervous about my skills on the ice. I knew I was good. What I was scared about was exposing myself to my classmates in a way they had never seen me before. It was one thing to be a spectacle in front of eight-year-old boys who didn't even live in my town; it was another to expose myself to people I saw every day.

In school I was still pretty much a wallflower and tried as much as possible to blend into the background. It was my defense against the possibility of social rejection. If no one really paid attention to me, then they really couldn't hurt me or make me feel bad. But here I was, thinking about putting myself directly in front of all the people I was trying to hide from and

I was afraid I would skate out on the ice for tryouts and they would take one look at me and say, "You're kidding." That was my greatest fear: not being taken seriously at the one thing in my life I did take seriously.

In the end, my need to play competitive hockey on the high school level forced me to put aside my fears. There were ten goalies trying out for the team that year, and the team was only picking two to play. I didn't make it . . . but I wasn't devastated. I had played okay during tryouts and I felt I had opened up some eyes, even if there were some people saying some not-very-flattering things about me. At least I had Racquet and Rink to go back to.

When I was a senior in high school, I tried out again. That year the competition was even stiffer, with twelve goalies trying out, but I felt I had improved a lot over the last year, and I thought I did well during the tryouts. After we were all done, I went into the ladies' room to change—there was no women's locker room at the rink—and there was a knock at the door. It was the coach and manager asking if they could come in and speak with me for a minute. I was still in my hockey gear, all sweaty, and I didn't know what was going on. Usually they announced the team roster in front of everyone who tried out. We exchanged a couple of awkward jokes about them being in the ladies' room and then they got down to business. I saw they had smiles on their faces. They said, "We wanted to tell you alone. You made the team. You're going to back up Mike Alloco"—the starting goalie.

Well, I will never forget that feeling. It was the best feeling I had ever had, and the first words out of my mouth were, "I'm not going to let you down." Even back then I knew, as bold a move as it was for me to try out for the boys' ice hockey team, it was an even bolder move for them to accept me. Some people say I've broken a lot of ground and helped pave the way for women in a male-dominated industry, but I know that at almost every barrier I broke, there was a bold man in a position of power standing there who recognized my potential and was willing to take a personal risk to give me an opportunity.

That whole year was great, but my shining moment came early in the season—and it pretty much changed everything. Mike, as usual, had started in goal and was really getting hammered by the other team. Mike was a great goalie, but it was just one of those games. By the middle of the second period, we were losing 5–2. The coach put me in just to give Mike a break, but putting me in changed the momentum of the game. I don't know if they were just shocked to see me in the net or what, but, I was able to stop everything they fired at me. With the end of the period coming up, we were tied 5–5. With just two minutes left in the game, both teams were battling for the puck at center ice when one of the opposing players skated toward me on a breakaway. He was coming down the ice as fast as he could, and I knew if he scored we would probably lose the game and I might not get a chance to play in another game for a while. I figured he was going to try to deke me, but I left a little extra room on my glove side, which was my strength, hoping he would take the bait, which he did. At about 8 feet out, he fired a wrist shot—and I snapped it out of the air with my glove like it was nothing.

My team went crazy and they all came down to give me a tap on my pads. We went on to score another goal in regulation to win the game, but, as much as I loved it, the win was a secondary victory to me. I knew the way I performed during that game showed my coach and manager that they had made the right decision in letting me play. I also knew that, in that period and a half, I had proven to my teammates that I knew what I was doing and could be an asset to their team.

After that game, Mike and I traded off starts for the rest of the season; I won about half of my games. In school my team-mates hung out with the hot girls and didn't even notice me if I passed them in the hall. On the ice, though, it was a different story. During most games, players from the opposing team would want to get their crack at intimidating the girl in the net, but I would have none of it. I modeled my style after Eddie Giacomin and Billy Smith (yes, the Islander), and I wasn't afraid to start a scuffle by pushing a player back with my stick if he tried to crowd me. Whenever that happened, I had five knights in shin-ing armor rushing to my aid. They trusted me and depended on me and they weren't going to let anyone mess with their goalie, even if I was a girl. Wow!

Although my teammates didn't see me as anything but a goalie, I had my eye on a couple of the guys. There was one guy in particular, Ray, whom I really liked. He was the manager's son, one of the best players on the team—and I thought he was really hot. He came to my defense whenever I needed him and was always the first to tap my pads when I made a good save. I wish I could tell you the story about how I dreamed he would ask me to the senior prom, but that wasn't even a glimmer of hope in my mind. I don't know who he ended up taking to the prom, but I'm pretty sure *I* ended up in front of the TV with Hank watching a baseball game and eating a linzer torte.

As the school year ended, I started looking forward to going away to college. I had applied to a number of state schools and ended up picking the State University College at Oswego. It was a beautiful campus right on the shores of New York State's Lake Ontario and was supposed to have been rated by *National Geographic* as having the second most beautiful sunsets in the world; the most beautiful were somewhere in Japan. Oswego also had a reputation for having a very friendly student body and was sometimes referred to in brochures as "The Friendly College on the Lake." It was also sometimes called "Oz." I didn't know what that meant, but I thought it was cool.

Regardless of what it was called, it goes without saying that the school I picked had a women's ice hockey team. It also had a communications/broadcasting department. I was only seventeen at the time and really had no idea what I was going to do with my life, but I knew I wanted to stand out, work in sports, or both. I loved music, so being a DJ was a possibility. So was working in sports PR. I didn't really know.

What I did know was that I was looking forward to going to a place where nobody had any preconceived notions about who I was or what I was like. I had changed a lot in the last few years—I had shed my glasses, proven myself as a hockey player, and become more confident overall—and I was ready to show everyone the real Linda I felt had always been hiding inside.

One quick word about the Talking Couch before we move past my childhood, because, well, I promised you I would, and I think it will help give you some perspective on the rest of my life. In my home, in the living room in which we were never allowed, there was a couch that nobody ever sat on, except in times of emotional turmoil. We called it the Talking Couch.

It was where my mother would sit down with each of us to solve our deepest and most serious problems. When I sat on the couch, it was usually because I was sad and lonely or to discuss my self-esteem issues. That doesn't come as a surprise, does it?

As I got older, my mother started using the couch to prepare me for college. She continued to instill within me the belief that I could do anything I put my mind to, and she was always trying to boost up my confidence by telling me what a wonderful and, of course, beautiful girl I was. She also offered me what she saw as the two basic principles of love. Get ready; this may not be what you expect:

❖ The first lesson my mother taught me was a fairy tale with a moral of sorts. She told me that when she was in college, there were many men who wanted to marry her. A number of them were very handsome, and she admitted to being more in love with several of them than she was with my father. She settled for Hank, though, because she thought he would make a better father. I never really understood the value of telling your daughter that her father was second best, but there it was.

❖ The second lesson was more straightforward: "Make sure the man you marry loves you more than you love him." What the—?

So there I was, armed with the two basic tenets of my mother's philosophy on life and love and, ready or not, headed for the Land of Oz.

TWO

The Land of Oz

During my first week on campus at Oswego, I was jogging down by Lake Ontario, trying to get in shape for the tennis team, when I stopped by a group of students standing in a grassy clearing watching the sunset. Like me, they all seemed to have been on their way to somewhere else when they noticed the sun setting over the lake. It was my first Oswego sunset . . . and it was breathtaking. The sky had a slight overcast to it, and as the sun began to sink below the horizon, it cast layers of yellow, orange, and red across the sky. No one spoke a word, and when the sun finally set, we all broke into spontaneous applause. It was a magical moment for me and it filled me with the feeling that I would be spending four wonderful and magical years at Oswego.

The sunset, you see, had made me completely forget about my two roommates who, for reasons beyond my own simple understanding, seemed to hate my guts almost as soon as they met me. The situation was so bad that, when we were all in the room together, Renee and Stacy would sit and talk to each other as if I weren't there. If I came back from classes and they were both already there, they usually wouldn't even raise their heads or say a word when I came in and said hi. It got to the point where the only time I would go to my room was to sleep. I'm not sure why they didn't like me, but I think the fact I was out playing sports and not around all the time to be part of their little sisterhood—they seemed to do *everything* together— didn't help.

Whatever the reason, it didn't matter much to me. Well, okay, it did matter, a lot. But I wasn't the timid little wallflower I had been throughout most of high school anymore, and I wasn't going to just sit around and feel sorry for myself. There was a girl, Nancy, on the seventh floor of Hart Hall, the dorm I lived in, whom I knew vaguely from high school field hockey, and I started hanging out with her and her friends.

On seventh-floor Hart, we did pretty much what everybody else did at Oswego. We ate in the dining hall and we drank everywhere else (back then the drinking age was eighteen). We drank in our rooms, we drank at parties, we drank at the College Tavern, and we drank at any one of the supposedly 153 bars in town. Maybe that's why Oswego was known as "The Friendly College on the Lake."

One of the reasons Oswego was such a big drinking school was its almost unbearable winters. Although the Oswego campus was green, beautiful, and full of days ending with breathtaking sunsets when I arrived in late August, seemingly overnight it turned into a vast, snowy wasteland. Oswego is located in an area of New York called the Snow Belt, and the town itself is known as the Buckle on the Snow Belt. The saying was that it could snow in any month with an *r* in it.

How much snow was there? Well, when I came back from winter break in my freshman year, it snowed every day for thirty-three days. The snow banks along the side of the road grew to more than 7 feet tall, and the town was using flatbed freight train cars to ship the snow south. Along with the snow came the wind off the lake, which could get so fierce that, every winter, the college put ropes up along the walking paths closest to the water to stop students from being blown away. So you see, the snow and wind really didn't leave us with much to do except drink, or fall in love. I did both.

The very first romance of my life was with Chris. He was a senior, and we met in the back row of Psych 101. Don't ask me what a senior was doing in a psychology class full of freshmen; I wasn't really thinking about that at the time. What I was thinking about was, here was a senior, a man of experience who probably had his pick of women, who seemed really interested in me. In my world, if you were really interested in *me,* then I was really interested in *you.* If not, then that was your loss. Good attitude, huh? In addition to really liking me, what attracted me to Chris was that he was going through his own little personal drama, and, with my family background, I could definitely relate to drama.

Chris had just broken up with his girlfriend of four years (warning number one), whom he had been dating since high school (warning number two), and who lived in my dorm (warning number three). All the warning signs were there, but, to me, it just made him seem genuine and deep and all of that kind of stuff. He also talked to me all the time about how depressed he was over the breakup (could that have been warning number four?). I never noticed that red flag, though, because I was convinced I could cure Chris of his heartache and, as one of the popular Pablo Cruise songs of the time said, teach him to "learn to love again." Oh yeah, what was I thinking?

Despite the obvious warning signs, we hit it off right away. After a few classes of talking and laughing in hushed tones at the back of the lecture hall—I always hung out in the back of the lecture hall because, well, learning was my priority—we began going to meals together. Unfortunately, whenever we were in the dining hall, it seemed his ex-girlfriend was a table or two away giving me the evil eye. I didn't know what her problem was, since *she* had broken up with *him*—at least that's what Chris said. Just the same, it was pretty awkward for us in the dining hall, so Chris and I started hanging out more in his room to get away from prying eyes. Somehow my roommates managed to get along without me.

Speaking of my loving roommates, the relationship between us got worse and worse, if that's possible. They seemed to have gone from just hating my guts to really detesting me. Finally I had to do something. I went to my RA and told her I wanted to switch rooms. I expected her to give me a hard time and tell me getting along with other people was part of going to college. I knew it wasn't easy for a freshman to switch rooms in the middle of first semester, but I couldn't stand it anymore. I had to get out.

To my surprise, my RA told me Renee and Stacy had been asking her if they could kick me out for weeks. At the time, I was completely taken by surprise, but, looking back, I have to admit I probably came off to them as self-centered and even a little bitchy. That was partly due to my residual shyness and the fact that, well, I was a little self-centered, but not to the point that it justified treating me like I wasn't there. Whatever the reason, I was as happy to be rid of them as they were to be rid of me. There was a girl, Cathy, on the seventh floor, where I was hanging out, who needed a roommate, so I moved in with her. Somehow she was able to put up with me for the whole rest of the year.

About the same time I was escaping the hell of Renee and Stacy, hockey practice was starting up. In the late 1970s women's ice hockey was still in its infancy, and we had quite a ragtag team. Some of the players, like our co-captains, Anne Potter and Heidi Hack, were among the best in our division. Most, though, had never played hockey before, and there was a good third of them who hadn't even known how to skate when they joined the team. Obviously, I could relate, but it appeared a few of them were never going to learn how to skate no matter how long they played.

Before I even stepped into the rink, I had a reputation to live up to. Everyone on the team had heard that I used to play on my high school boys' team, and expectations were high. I wasn't worried, though. I much preferred to be in a position where I had to live up to high expectations than one in which I had to prove someone's low expectations of me were wrong. I was proud of my accomplishments on the ice, and I knew I could stand up to my reputation.

One thing I wasn't so proud of was the rumor going around the team that my high school grades hadn't been good enough to get me into Oswego. People were saying some strings had been pulled to get me accepted so I could play on the team. I was pretty sure it was more than a rumor. Oswego was the best school I had applied to, and I had never really expected to get in. While to this day, no one at Oswego will come right out and admit it, unofficially I think I was the first dumb female jock to get an athletic admission there.

Back in those days, most of the girls who had any exposure or interest at all to playing hockey hailed from central or upstate New York. My appearance, I later found out, was not what my new teammates had expected of a goalie—especially one tough enough to play on the boys' team. The women on the team were, for the most part, Ivory girl types who wore no makeup and used dryers on their hair only to stop it from freezing up in the cold Oswego wind after a shower. In comparison, I was a Long Island girl who had only recently decided she wasn't a total ugly duckling and usually had on so much makeup, it looked like I'd put it on with a paintbrush. You know what I'm talking about, lots of blush and eyeliner and mascara. As for my hair, I would usually spend at least twenty minutes drying, straightening, fluffing, and then curling it into feathered wingbacks that framed my face. Hey, that was how they wore it on Long Island back then.

In addition to my appearance, I had an outward personality that, at first glance, definitely did not spell out *competitive hockey player.* As I've already mentioned, I had never thought of myself as very smart, and it showed. I came off as dumb and flighty—what was referred to back then as an airhead: I talked very loud, inexplicably drawing attention to myself, and when I spoke, I came off as unsure, often saying something off topic or that didn't make much sense. Also, I laughed almost constantly—actually it was more like an uncontrollable giggle—and I laughed at everything, even things other people didn't think were funny. I like to think I just had a very sophisticated sense of humor, but maybe I really was just an airhead.

So, I guess I got a few strange looks when I met with my new teammates for the first time, but I was too naive and too excited to finally be playing hockey with girls to notice. During that first practice, I went through the regular drills and took some shots from my teammates, but nothing too challenging. I could tell they were beginning to accept the possibility that someone who looked and acted like me might actually be able to play hockey, but they didn't seem quite ready to accept me as the great hope they had heard of. As usual, I didn't care. I knew I would prove myself to them in time and I knew Rich, my coach, knew it too. I could be patient.

Near the end of our practice, the men's team suited up and came out to watch us. When our practice was over, Rich said to Herb Hammond, the men's coach who was instrumental in recruiting me to Oswego, "Hey, Herb, why don't you let the guys take a few shots on Linda."

So the guys took the ice and began lobbing easy shots at me. When they saw I was a little underwhelmed by their efforts, they upped the intensity of their shots until they were giving me everything they had. I responded by giving them everything I had, butterflying or making pretty amazing glove saves for just about every shot. That, I think, is when I earned the respect of my team. Anne, one of the co-captains, later said to me, "I remember the first time you came onto the ice and we weren't too sure about you. You definitely didn't look or act like a goalie to us. Then the guys came out and were taking real shots at you, and you were dropping down to stop them and making real saves. We had never seen anything like that from a girl before. That's when I knew we had our goalie. That's when I knew we had our Cohn-Head!"

Cohn-Head, that's what Anne called me—after the *Saturday Night Live* skit with Dan Aykroyd and Jane Curtin—and the name stuck. I have to tell you, in my entire life, there has never been a more elating experience than skating out on the ice at the beginning of a game and having all of my teammates banging their sticks against the boards and yelling out, "Cohn-Head!"

But that was just the icing on the cake. The best part was that I was finally playing hockey with other women, and I loved it. Win or lose, playing on the road, or playing on our home ice in a converted army barracks with lousy lighting, no heat, and not one hockey fan in the stands, it was the greatest feeling in the world. I loved playing with these girls because *I* loved playing hockey and *they* loved playing hockey and, like me, they played with every ounce of energy and determination they had.

Each and every one of them had the heart of a true hockey player: from Anne, who had come to Oswego to play basketball but was so drawn to the hockey team that she decided to spend the sixty dollars she had saved for a new pair of basketball shoes on a pair of reconditioned hockey skates; through Heidi Hack, who was born without ligaments in one of her shoulders and would dislocate it every few games and have to wait in agonizing pain until Anne could skate over to her and force it back into place; to Sarah, who would fall down on the ice for no reason other than she couldn't skate to save her life, but would just pick herself up and get back in the game. I loved playing with all of them, and it was one of the greatest experiences of my life.

Then there was Rich, our coach. He was a former Oswego hockey player himself, and the best coach I've ever had. He didn't treat us like girls who played hockey; he just treated us like hockey players who happened to be girls. He taught us to dig deep for that extra effort, and he taught us how to be winners, even when the scoreboard said otherwise. No matter what happened during the game, we always went out to celebrate afterward—and as good a hockey coach as Rich was, he was even better at teaching us how to celebrate. Unfortunately, I can't tell you any of those celebratory stories without getting some innocent people in trouble. Let's just say Rich really knew how to make us feel like a team, and leave it at that.

In addition to playing hockey, hanging with my new friends on seventh-floor Hart, and spending a whole lot of time with Chris, I went to the library as often as I could to study. Well, that's a lie. I did spend a lot of time in the library, but you couldn't really call what I was doing studying. I always went to the library intending to study, but most of the time it didn't work out that way.

My biggest problem with the library was that it had a music room filled with turntables, headphones, and thousands of records you could listen to for free! (Remember, this was before iPods and music downloads.) I figured if I was going to study in the library, I might as well do it while I was listening to music. I spent hours in that room with a textbook or notebook in my lap, pretending to myself that I was studying when I was actually paying a lot more attention to the music I was listening to and thinking about what album I was going to listen to next.

As midterms approached, I started getting more serious about studying and abandoned the music room for one of the study carrels in the main section of the library. The library had three floors connected by a broad central staircase. There were carrels on each floor, but I always made sure to pick one on the first floor, right by the staircase. This put me in the perfect position to see who was coming in and out of the library. No surprise here: I ended up doing a lot more socializing than studying. I was making up for lost time.

One night I decided to reserve an individual study room in the library to cram for a particularly difficult test. These study rooms were small, private boxes, about 4 by 5 by 7 feet. They came with all the amenities you would expect to be given to someone desperate enough to need an individual study room: a desk, a chair, and an overhead fluorescent light. It was more like solitary confinement than a place where someone like me could study. That first and only time I reserved a study carrel, I lasted fifteen minutes before I packed up my books and ran downstairs to my sanctuary, the music room. I managed to pass the test, but just barely.

A few days after midterms, just before Thanksgiving break, Chris came to my room, sat down next to me on my bed, and told me he was going back to his old girlfriend. Not much of a surprise now, but at the time I was totally caught off guard. Although we had only been seeing each other for a couple of months, I really thought we had a love that was meant to be. I was pitiful. You know, for weeks I had been walking around with that stupid Pablo Cruise song in my head, but now I had a new song—"Emotion" by the Bee Gees—ricocheting through my brain. And it wasn't making me feel any better, because this song talked about a sorrow that will never go away and the pain of wondering who your former love is holding now.

I know you think I'm making this music stuff up, but I'm not. Sure, on the outside, I seemed more or less like a typical, moderately functional freshman—but inside my head I lived in a little fantasy world where true love happened just like it did in the movies, and the songs I heard on the radio were the soundtrack of my own life.

The lyrics of "Emotion" were especially poignant to me because I knew exactly who Chris was holding every night instead of me. In fact, I saw her sitting with him, talking and laughing during every meal in the dining hall. She seemed to revel in the fact that I now had to watch her. Looking at them, I thought, *What a cruel twist of fate.*

For the rest of the semester, I spent a lot of time feeling sorry for myself and thinking I would never get over this misery. My less-than-three-months with Chris seemed like a lifetime, and I was never going to be the same. Luckily, when I went back home at the end of the semester, something happened to help me take my mind off Chris. I got my grades in the mail, and they were not good.

For my first semester at college, I got a 1.8. That put me on academic probation and in danger of getting kicked out of school at the end of the next semester. I knew I wasn't very smart, but this was really bad. I was a communications major and I had gotten a D in Introduction to Broadcasting and a C in Intro to Mass Media. I had a D+ average in my major. My future in broadcasting looked bright.

Needless to say, I spent a lot less time in the music room during the second semester and I managed to get my grades up.* With my grades safely improved and the end of the year coming, I started looking forward to my sophomore year. I got a new roommate—Barb—and we ended up with a room on the fourth floor. Hart was being converted into a coed dorm over

---

* Just for the record, I earned a 3.6 my last semester at Oswego. Maybe I wasn't that dumb after all.

the summer, so there were half as many rooms available for girls and most of them were going to upperclassmen. Barb was a senior, though, so we had no trouble getting in.

Over the summer I worked at Burger King and gained fifteen pounds by taking advantage of the 20 percent employee discount. Luckily, I had still been pretty skinny, and most of those pounds moved into the right places. In August I headed back to school, looking forward to another year at Oswego. With a year under my belt, I felt I pretty much knew what to expect from school and was better prepared to deal with it: same school, same major, same friends, same dorm, and same teammates. The only differences were that I was on a different floor, and Hart was now coed. I didn't expect either of these changes to have much of an impact on me, but I was mistaken. They were going to change my life.

The very first day I came back to Oswego for my sophomore year, I was unpacking when two guys I had never seen before knocked on my door. I thought, *Hey, I'm going to like living in a coed dorm.* Don't get all excited, though—as it turns out, they were knocking on everyone's door to invite us to a get-acquainted party in their room later that night.

I told them I was going out with my friends—I had a whole bunch now—and one of them said, "Well, you can stop by when you come back. I'm sure the party will still be going on."

I thought to myself that there weren't going to be any parties still going on by the time *I* got back, but to be polite I said, "Okay. Maybe I will." After all, they were both kind of cute.

That night I went out with some of my old friends, and at some point we started talking about what we were going to do when we graduated. It was a pretty strange conversation for a bunch of Oswego students in the late '70s, and I was barely paying attention. But then one of my friends, Shari, turned to me and said, "Linda, what are you going to do when you get out of school?"

Without even thinking, I said, "In a perfect world, I would like to be a sports broadcaster."

The words were out of my mouth before I even knew I had said them. Inside me, a little voice said *Ooops!* Because in a world where there was not a single female sportscaster on TV or the radio, I had just told my friends that I—a dumb jock from Long Island who had just gotten off academic probation—was going to do something no female had ever done before. Then the little voice came back and, very quietly, said, *Oh,* because that was the first time I had admitted even to myself that I wanted to spend my life on the air talking about sports.

It was crazy, but hey, I had played hockey on the boys' high school team; why couldn't I be a sportscaster? After that, Shari and my friend Alison, who was also with us that night, loved to jokingly introduce me to someone new by saying, "This is Linda. She plays ice hockey and she's going to be a sportscaster." Most people, of course, didn't take them seriously, and I myself never mentioned it to anyone again. It really was too crazy an idea.

I got back to the dorm a little after midnight and, sure enough, the get-acquainted party was still going on. In fact, it was going strong. The party had spilled out into the hallway, and everyone was laughing and having a great time. Most of these people had not even known each other until that night, but, based on how they were acting, you would have thought this was a reunion rather than a get-acquainted party.

When I got to the party, the first person I ran into was Stew. It was Stew and his roommate, John, who had knocked on my door earlier that day and were hosting the party. We reintroduced ourselves and he said, "Oh yeah, you play field hockey, don't you?"

Field hockey. Oh great. I got this a lot.

When I explained to him that, no, I played *ice* hockey, he said, "Oh, I didn't even know Oswego had a girls' ice hockey team."

Wonderful.

You could be sure I wasn't going to be sharing my new revelation about wanting to become a sportscaster with this guy.

Usually when a conversation with a guy went in the direction of my being on the women's ice hockey team, the next line was something like, "Oh, I gotta go get a beer, see ya later." I know it's hard to believe but, being a female hockey player didn't usually enhance my appeal to the opposite sex. At the very least, the guy didn't want to be with a girl who might be a better athlete than he was. At worst, there was the whole "What type of girl actually plays ice hockey anyway?" thing; not that there's anything wrong with that, unless you want to get to know a guy better. Then it's usually a showstopper. But I quickly realized that it was different with Stew. He wasn't threatened or turned off by my being a jock; he actually seemed interested in what I was doing and what I had to say.

I know you know what's coming next. He was interested in me, so I was interested in him. But it was more than that. He had this unassuming way about him that put me completely at ease. He wasn't trying to impress me, or size me up, or figure out whether or not he was going to be able to get into my pants. He was just trying to get to know me better. And he was very funny. I don't remember what we talked about, but I remember laughing at everything he said. Yeah, I know, I laughed at everything anybody said anyway, but he really was funny.

Interestingly, his look was the complete opposite of the muscular athlete I thought I was always looking for (think *male hockey player*). Stew was tall and lean with a shaggy mop of hair and he had this kind of unintentional rock musician thing going on—kind of like Jackson Browne or Tom Scholz from Boston. (Hey, those guys were really big back then.) We talked for a long time, and I felt we had made a connection. That night, when I finally went to bed, I was still thinking about him.

It turned out I wasn't the only one thinking about Stew. I found out the next day that one of my new floormates, Lisa, was also interested in him. And over the next few weeks, I learned that Stew and his roommate, John, both attracted interest from a wide variety of women. A couple of days after the party, there was a stream of cute little freshman girls running in and out of their room. And the following Saturday night, there was a girl in Stew's bed promising him sexual favors if he would just come over and warm her up.

There were more, but it was all a lot less lurid than it sounds. John had a longtime girlfriend living in the room directly above him, and the girl in Stew's bed was just a friend who had had too much to drink and ended up saying a little more than she had meant to. Nonetheless, it was clear that if I wanted to get closer to Stew, I was going to have to beat out the competition.

That was okay with me. I loved competition and I was up to the task.

That first get-acquainted party had set a precedent and, over the next few weeks, all of us on the floor started spending a lot of time together. Another thing contributing to the closeness of the floor was that the TV in the so-called TV lounge never worked. Unlike most other TV lounges in the dorm, where people sat and watched TV alone and in a catatonic state, our TV lounge became a place to socialize. It seemed that, day or night, there was always at least a small group of people sitting there whenever I got off the elevator.

So, instead of just heading to my room when I got back from classes, I would usually walk into the TV lounge and hang out. We all got to know and like each other pretty well. After just a few weeks, when the weekend came around, I would check out what "the floor" was doing before making plans with anyone else. Another motivation I had for hanging out with my floor-mates was that I had a much better chance of running into Stew if I did.

My strategy worked. I started running into Stew a lot and I could see he really did like me. At this same time I became close friends with Dana. We became two peas in a pod because, while I liked Stew, Dana liked John. Unfortunately for Dana, John's girlfriend was naturally blond, cute, and a 4.0 student, and she and John had been going out for more than two years. Nothing against Dana, but the chances that John was going to break up with his girlfriend for her were zero to none.

That didn't stop Dana from trying, and the two of us would constantly scheme ways to spend more time with Stew and John. We did anything we could think of. We baked cookies (even though neither one of us had ever baked before in our lives), we gave them candy at Halloween, and we were always asking them to help us with one thing or another. You know, the damsel-in-distress thing.

Things went along like this for quite a while. Stew and I became close friends, but it never progressed beyond that. Even though Stew was very popular, I was beginning to see that he really was kind of hesitant when it came to romance. I didn't know if it was because he'd had a bad experience or if he was just a little shy, but I was going to figure out how to push him along.

One day, when we were all hanging out in the TV lounge, I mentioned to everyone that my birthday was coming up—you know *I* wasn't hesitant about trying to be the center of attention. Stew said, "Hey, that's a Friday, we can go to the College Tavern for happy hour! My treat." Stew was always going out of his way to do special things for me, but this looked like he was trying to bridge the gap between friendship and something more.

Just my luck, I couldn't go to happy hour with Stew and the rest of the floor because I had a hockey game that night. It was one of the few times I wished I didn't play hockey. When you're turning nineteen and you can't go out on your birthday with the guy you really like because of a hockey game, it changes your perspective.

I thought about calling my new coach, Pat, and telling her I was too sick to play, but I knew I couldn't do that. I was the only goalie. If I couldn't let my high school field hockey team down on Yom Kippur, how could I let my college ice hockey team down because it was my birthday? I was screwed.

That Friday I turned nineteen without much fanfare. I went through my usual day until I ran into Anne Potter a little after lunch.

"Hey Cohn-Head! Did you hear what happened?"

I said, "No. What?"

I wasn't expecting much of anything special, but Anne said, "The ice melted. The hockey game is canceled."

I thought she was making fun of me. I had told her about Stew, and she was always teasing me about him. Besides, in the entire history of hockey at Oswego, no one could ever remember the ice melting before. Really, whoever heard of a hockey game being canceled because the ice melted?

When I got back to fourth floor later that day, nobody could believe my luck. Ever since then, whenever something really lucky happens to me, I think of it as the ice melting.

So with luck now going my way, we all headed down to the College Tavern for happy hour. By 4:15 p.m. everyone was buying me drinks and I was showing off the shot-drinking skills I had learned from being on the hockey team. I was having a great time, of course, because it was my birthday, I was the center of attention, and Stew was there.

Just before 6:00 p.m. we ran over to catch dinner before the dining hall closed. Stew found out I had never seen the movie *Animal House* (it had just come out at the end of the summer), and he insisted I couldn't end my birthday without seeing it. Spending two hours in a dark movie theater with Stew didn't sound too horrible, so I agreed.

Stew borrowed his friend's car and he, Dana, and I drove off to the theater, which was a couple of miles outside town. Yeah, Stew, Dana, and me. So it wasn't the romantic interlude I had hoped for, but I laughed through the whole movie (what a surprise) and we had a good time—even though we were stopped for running a red light on the way home (we thought it was yellow). By this time, it was five hours since we had left the College Tavern; we think the cop was so surprised to find three Oswego college students out on a Friday night who were stone-cold sober, he let us off.

With my hopes for a romantic twosome on my birthday foiled, things didn't actually get to the "next level" with Stew and me until finals week. The evening had started with a bunch of us hanging out in the TV lounge, but before we knew it everyone else had left to go to sleep and it was just Stew and me. I was wearing one of those white, gauzy hippie shirts that were popular back then, and I knew I was looking pretty good.

We were sitting next to each other on one of the sofas and talking, but I was having trouble keeping track of the conversation. I kept stumbling over my words and I could feel my heart racing a little bit. Stew was stumbling over his words too. Then we both stopped talking and were just looking at each other. We were both breathing hard.

The next thing I remember, we were on the floor. I'm not sure how long we were there, but I remember hearing the elevator doors open and close several times and I knew we were easily visible through the glass doors. This wasn't the first time a couple had been seen in the TV lounge entwined in the throes of passion. A number of so-called romances had begun, and often ended, late at night in the TV lounge. Usually fourth floor Hart was abuzz with gossip the next day. I knew they'd be talking about us, but I just didn't care. I knew this was different. I bet that's what all those other couples thought too when they were rolling around the TV lounge floor, but I knew I was right about this.

Or maybe I was wrong. After our night in the lounge, everything seemed to go back to the way it had been. The next day Stew didn't mention it, or act any differently toward me than he ever had. I didn't know what to think. Did he think it was a mistake? Was he embarrassed? Was he confused? Or maybe it was just because it was finals week and we were all busy cramming to pass our tests. I just didn't know.

After a week of emotional limbo and late-night studying, it was time to get ready for the six-hour trip back home for winter break. Dana and I were traveling together, and we decided we would stop by Stew and John's room to say good-bye. John wasn't there, so Dana gave Stew a hug and then discreetly disappeared.

I didn't know what I was going to do, but I knew I had to do something. I couldn't stand not knowing what was going on. I walked up to Stew to give him a hug and then, at the last second, I changed my mind and pushed on his chest gently, but with a take-charge attitude, so he had to step backward into his room. I kicked the door shut with my foot, wrapped my arms around him, and gave him a big, long, wet kiss. It was the right thing to do. I stepped back and Stew had this dreamy look in his eyes. He said, "I guess I'll have to call you over the break."

"I guess you will," I said. Then I gave him a big smile and walked away. Smooth.

During winter break, Stew did call me and we set a date to go to a wine-and-cheese place not far from my house. I'm not going to go through the details of the date with you because, frankly, it was a bore. We drank some wine, ate some cheese, and ran out of things to say early in the evening. Stew drove me home, and as he pulled up in front of my house he said, "When can I see you again?"

I said, "You know, it just wasn't that great. I think I was more interested in just getting to the point where we were going out than anything else. It was the challenge of it. Now that we've actually gone out, I'm ready to move on to something else."

Do you believe it? After a whole semester of scheming, flirting, and, by the way, really getting to know and like Stew, I was ready to call the whole thing off after one date. You're probably thinking Stew yelled a couple of choice words at me, kicked me out of the car, and then drove off in a trail of smoke and screeching rubber, but that's not what happened. He was definitely confused and more than a little upset, but he agreed our date had been boring.

Then he said, "That's just the opposite of how I feel. I spent so much time figuring out how I felt about you. Now that I finally know how I feel, I don't want to let you go. I really like you and I think we could have something special. We shouldn't just end it because of one date that wasn't that good."

This little speech, as unpolished as it was, really made an impact. Stew, who never got upset and always went with the flow, was fighting for me. We talked some more about it and I decided it was a little crazy to break things off after everything we'd been through. We sealed the evening with a kiss, or maybe more than one, and ended up seeing a lot of each other over the break. By the time we got back to school, things were going really well. Over the next few months, I was thinking, not only is Stew a great boyfriend, he's my *best* friend.

In fact, back at school *everything* seemed to be going really well. My grades were up, our hockey team looked like it was on its way to a winning season, and I was getting involved with the campus radio station.

It was during this time with the station that I received a piece of advice from Fritz Messere, one of my communications professors, that would forever alter the path of my career. Growing up on eastern Long Island, and having a mother from Boston, I developed what could probably best be described as a Long Island accent on steroids. I had all the worst characteristics of a Long Island dialect—the exaggerated *g*, as in *lawnguyland* instead of *Long Island;* the missing *r*, as in *beeh* instead of *beer;* and the missing *aw* sound that they never allowed into Boston—*wottah* instead of *water* and *cot* instead of *caught.*

This really made me stand out on campus radio, and not in a good way. In the broadcasting business, what they euphemistically call "regionalism" is very bad. While there are a few notable exceptions, most people with an accent don't go very far in radio or on TV. I couldn't hear my own accent (which was part of the problem), but I knew it was really bad because even my Long Island friends would tease me about it.

My professors, and the advisers at the radio station, would also warn me that if I wanted to be on the air professionally, I would have to lose my accent. However, other than suggesting years of intensive linguistics retraining, they were hard pressed to tell me how. Only Fritz was able to give me a very simple solution, and I tell you about it now only because you, or someone you know, may be able to take advantage of this little piece of advice someday. What Fritz said to me was: "Talk more slowly and open your mouth wider when you speak."

It sounded simple, but it really worked, and it really did alter my chances of success in broadcasting, although it had a milder affect on my off-air voice. I'm kind of at the point now where I can almost turn it on or off at will. I don't think one voice is more genuine than the other; they just show two different sides of my personality. When I'm relaxed, or when I'm having a one-on-one conversation, the accent comes out more. When I'm on the air, trying to give my audience the most complete and understandable information I can in the shortest amount of time, the accent tends to go away. Even now, upon meeting me in person for the first time, I still sometimes hear people say, "Oh, I didn't know you were from Long Island." That's just fine. I'm proud of who I am and I don't try to hide it.

Getting back to my sophomore year, everything seemed to be going well. Everything, that is, except my contact lenses.

Because my prescription was so strong, and because I had an astigmatism as well, my contact lenses were relatively thick and big—sort of the contact-lens version of my old tortoise-shell glasses. If you looked carefully at my eyes, you could see that the lenses extended about a millimeter beyond my irises, and they were thick enough that you could spot a lump in the center of my eye if you caught me from the side. As a result, ever since I'd gotten my first set of contact lenses, I'd had problems. Lately, though, they were getting worse. I often had uncontrollable tearing during class, and it seemed my eyes were always getting irritated to the point that I couldn't wear my contact lenses at all.

You know how I felt about wearing my glasses, so it shouldn't be a surprise for you to learn that, even with these problems, I never wore them. If my eyes hurt when I put my contact lenses in, I would just take out the one that hurt more and walk around with one contact lens.

That made actually seeing and getting around campus very difficult, but it was better than exposing the ugly duckling under the facade I felt I had created with my makeup, feathered-back hair, and contact lenses. I honestly thought if people saw me wearing glasses, they would completely change their opinion of me; my tenuous status in the college hierarchy would drop from a reasonably attractive, reasonably popular, fun-loving girl with a boyfriend to a pitiful outcast, left to spend her nights all alone in her room listening to sad songs. Just like high school.

The only time I would wear my glasses was if my lenses were completely unbearable to wear *and* I was in my room studying alone with the door closed.

With all the troubles I was having with my lenses, Stew thought I was being ridiculous. He would say that if I was in that much pain, I should just put my glasses on and no one would care. But he had never seen me with my glasses on, and I was going to make sure he never did.

"Do you think I'm going to care less about you if I see you with your glasses on? I'm your boyfriend. Just put them on. It doesn't matter to me."

"No" is all I would ever say.

Living next door to Stew was a guy named Martin. Martin was harmless, but, to put it bluntly, he was strange, didn't fit in very well, and didn't even try. Having had trouble myself once fitting in, I had an aversion to anyone else like that—sad but true.

There were a lot of things about Martin that were just a little bit concerning, but the one he was known all over campus for— and the one he was proudest of—was that he never wore a jacket when he went outside. Even in February, when the temperature was 20 degrees and the wind chill made it feel like 0, you would see him on his way to class in just a button-down shirt with the top two or three buttons open.

Martin would tell anyone who would listen, "I believe I can withstand the cold and regulate my internal body temperature through the power of my mind. If I tell myself I'm not cold, then I won't be cold."

Yeah right. What he didn't tell people was that the only way he was able to keep himself from freezing to death was by walking very, very, very fast to class and not stopping for any reason. If he did stop, his teeth would chatter and his legs would start shaking almost immediately.

As you might imagine, most people steered away from Martin. Everyone, that is, except for Stew and John, who lived next door to him and were just too nice to hurt his feelings. Because I was Stew's girlfriend, Martin felt a special closeness to me as well, and he would try to strike up a conversation whenever he saw me. For Stew, I put up with him the best I could.

As April's Fools' Day approached, I started thinking it would be fun to play a joke on Stew, and I knew just what I was going to do. Stew had a blue-and-white-striped shirt he looked great in, but that I had seen him wear only once. I was always asking him to wear it, and he was always telling me he didn't like it. I don't know why he didn't just throw it out and, as you'll see, it would have been better for both of us if he had.

Anyway, Stew and John never locked their door, so on April 1, when they were both out at dinner, Dana and I snuck into their room and stole every one of Stew's shirts—except, of course, for the one with the blue-and-white stripes.

After I hid Stew's shirts in Dana's room, I went back to my room. My contacts were really killing me that day and I had a big test to study for, so I shut my door, took out my contact lenses, and put my glasses on. That was a major tactical error on my part.

When Stew got back to his room, it didn't take long for him to notice that all of his shirts—except the one with the blue-and-white stripes—were missing. It took him even less time to figure out who had taken them.

I was sitting at my desk when Stew knocked on my door. I told him to come in and tried to act like nothing was going on. My desk faced away from the front door, so I could hide the big smile I just couldn't seem to wipe off my face, although I was laughing. I knew I had gotten him bad.

Stew came up behind me and put his hands on my shoulders. He was laughing too and told me I had pulled a great practical joke . . . and that now I could give him back his shirts. I turned to him with the sweetest, most loving look I could muster and said, "You're not getting your shirts back until you wear the one that's in your closet."

Stew tried to soften me up and get me to tell him where his shirts were. First, he told me he didn't think I looked that bad with my glasses on (he was one of the most honest people I've ever known, so he couldn't say I actually looked *good* with my glasses on). Then he started massaging my shoulders. It felt good, but there was no way I was going to give him his shirts back until he wore the one with the blue-and-white stripes. I held firm. Then, all of a sudden, he stopped rubbing my shoulders and said, "Okay, if that's the way it is, I'll see you later." He walked out, closing the door behind him.

I didn't know what he had up his sleeve, but I was pretty sure he wasn't running back to his room to put on the blue-and-white shirt. I sat there and waited for his next move. Then a lightbulb clicked on in my head. I turned around to look at the dresser behind me where I had left my contact lenses in their case. They were gone!

And I was trapped. Without my contact lenses, there was no way I was going to venture out of my room. I called Dana, and she came over to help me plan my next move. I explained that I couldn't leave the room with my glasses on and told her she would have to tell Stew I needed my contacts back.

She left on her sacred mission and came back a few minutes later, without my contacts. I said, "What happened?"

Dana said, "Nothing. They just laughed."

So there I was, left with no choice. I can't begin to tell you how mortified I was to be venturing out of my room with my glasses on, but I had to get my contact lenses back as soon as possible. I asked Dana to run defense for me, and we walked quickly down the hall, hoping to run into as few people as possible. Stew lived at the other end of the floor, and when we got there, he was sitting on the couch with John in the easy chair (they had a really nice room setup). When they saw us, they both started laughing.

I had to put up as good a front as possible.

I started laughing too, and I said, "I need my contacts."

Stew said, "Give me back my shirts and you'll get your contacts."

I ignored him. "I need my contacts. I can't go walking around with my glasses on. You know how I feel about that."

"Sure you can. What's the big deal?"

I said, "Look, I really need my contacts." I was still laughing, but I was really upset that people were going be seeing me with my glasses on.

Stew said, "It's very simple, give me my shirts back and I'll give you your contacts."

I said, "I can't do that," and Stew said, "Why not?'

"Because that would mean I lost."

Ah. That's what it really boiled down to. I could have easily ended this whole thing if I would just give Stew back his shirts. But there was no way I was going to admit that my boyfriend had beaten me at my own game.

That should have been a sign to Stew. He should have just run away from me and never looked back. He should have gone and found that girl who'd tried to seduce him into his own bed at the beginning of the semester. Or he should have looked to see if any of those freshmen girls who'd paraded through his room were still interested in him. Or he should have just given up girls altogether. Anything had to be more promising than a girlfriend who saw April Fools' Day as a way to get an upper hand on her boyfriend.

But Stew didn't run away. He just smiled and said, "You are never going to find your contact lenses unless you give me my shirts back. You can look all you want."

So we did. We looked between the sofa cushions, in the desk drawers, under the mattresses, everywhere—and I was beginning to think he was right. Then Martin, who had walked in a few minutes before to see what the commotion was, started to help us look. Martin, whom Stew had befriended out of the sheer goodness of his heart, betrayed him in the blink of an eye.

We had already searched Stew's closet—it was pretty easy since there was only one shirt in there—but there was a shelf all the way up at the top that we hadn't thought to check. We couldn't reach it anyway. Martin, who was about 5 foot 5, couldn't reach it either, so he started climbing up on the other shelves to get to it. I could see Stew was keeping a close eye on Martin, but he stayed leaned back on the couch. There was a box of Bounce fabric softener sheets on that upper shelf, and as soon as Martin reached for it, Stew leapt from the couch and jumped on Martin. They scrambled for the box. Stew ripped the box apart, pulled the contact lens case from inside the cardboard roll where it was hidden, and ran out the door, making a left. Martin took off after him.

I still don't understand why Martin was so intent on getting my contact lenses back for me, but there it was.

Our floor was shaped like a big rectangle divided in half by an elevator lobby. The boys lived to the right of the lobby and the girls were on the left. Stew ran down the hall, across the elevator lobby and into the girls' side of the floor with Martin right behind him. They ran around the girls' hall and when

Stew got to the far end, he grabbed the fire door that separated the hallway from the elevator lobby to pull it closed behind him. Just as he did so, Martin—who considered himself, among other things, to be an expert in martial arts—took a flying leap toward the door and tried to kick it shut.

Unfortunately, Stew was already partway through the door, so instead of kicking the door shut, Martin kicked it right into Stew's face. They both toppled to the ground. Martin scrambled over to see if Stew was all right. Then he started apologizing profusely. Stew slowly got to his feet, said "Yeah, I'm all right," and took off. Martin, I guess, was too upset to continue and gave up the chase.

A few minutes later Stew came back to his room, where we were all waiting for him. He was, apparently, not all right. He had a big split under his lip and was bleeding pretty badly. Despite the obvious pain, he was smiling, and I noticed right away that he did not have my contact lenses with him. I told you I had underestimated my opponent.

I was pretty upset. You know why. Not because Stew was hurt but because, after all that, I still didn't have my contact lenses. We decided Stew was bleeding badly enough for him to go to the health center to get things looked at, and he headed over there alone. Of course, I let him go over there by himself. There was no way I was going to walk across campus with my glasses on.

About an hour later Stew called to let me know they had taken him to the emergency room. He also told me where I could find my contact lenses: on the fifth floor, in his friend Mark's room. In the emergency room, they found a 1-millimeter piece of wood from the fire door in the cut under his lip and gave him six stitches. Then, when he finally came back at about 10:00 p.m., he had to pull an all-nighter because he hadn't even started a report that was due the next day.

What a mess. All I wanted to do was play a little joke and get Stew to wear my favorite shirt. Instead I got my joke turned around on me and my boyfriend's face slammed in a door. But none of that was what I was thinking about. What I really was thinking was: *I won!* After all, Stew *did* tell me where my contact lenses were before I gave him back his shirts.

Okay, I admit I was far from perfect, but the truth is, Stew was no gift either. Up until now, I've hidden a deep dark secret about him because I didn't want to admit to you that I was such a poor judge of character. But it's time to come clean. The deep, dark truth is that Stew hated sports! Well, he didn't exactly hate sports; it was just that he'd rather be doing anything else in the world than watch a sporting event on TV. What are the odds? Of all of the guys at Oswego, you have to figure I had better than a fifty–fifty chance of picking one who shared my enthusiasm. But no, I had to pick the *one* guy who couldn't care less if he never saw another sporting event in his life. And of all the games Stew didn't like, he didn't like hockey the most! Talk about warning signs. I'm the one that should have run away and never looked back.

The problem was, by the time I found out Stew was the anti-sports-fan, I had already fallen pretty hard for him. Oswego was a funny place when it came to sports. We didn't have a football team, and most of our other teams weren't all that good. It wasn't as if everyone else was going to our college games except for Stew. The men's hockey team was very good, but I wasn't going to those games anyway—I was usually playing on the road when the men had a game at home. Also, don't forget the TV in the TV lounge was broken, so I wasn't asking Stew to sit down with me and watch a Rangers game or anything. It almost seemed like there were some greater powers conspiring to get us together.

To his credit, Stew did his best to compensate for his one major character flaw. He went to every one of my home hockey games, even though they never turned on the heat at the rink for the women's games and despite usually being the only spectator in the stands. Over the summer we both stayed in Oswego, and he would watch the occasional Mets game with me. He had a hard time understanding how I could carry the depression of a loss with me all the way until the next game, but he put up with it. Overall, we were able to keep the potential volatility of a sports-fan/non-sports-fan relationship from turning into a full-blown nuclear explosion. That is, until Stew's twenty-first birthday.

Stew's birthday was in April, which meant it came during the most important time of the year for me: the Stanley Cup playoffs. It also meant that it fell just after spring break. Stew and I had traveled back up to school together that spring, and by the time we got back to the old, dilapidated house he was renting with John and a few other friends, it was early evening.

John had a new girlfriend whom we all liked—no, it wasn't Dana, it was a girl named Nancy—but that's a very long story that I'm not going to go into here—and it turned out that Nancy's birthday was the day after Stew's. As was usually the case at that house, when we arrived that evening, there were a bunch of people over, and an impromptu birthday celebration for Stew and Nancy broke out. I hung out with them for a while, but, to be honest, I was getting bored. Everyone was just sort of hanging out, and I kept wondering what was happening in the game (it was the first round of the playoffs, and the Rangers were playing the Atlanta Flames). While everyone else was laughing and drinking, I was thinking to myself, *I know I can get Marv Albert on the stereo in Stew's room.* So I wandered over there to find out.

I tuned into the station and, although the reception was a little staticky, I could definitely hear what was going on in the game. I was really excited and ran out to share my good fortune with Stew, who, in retrospect, seemed less than enthralled with my news, but I didn't notice at the time. The party was getting kind of noisy, so I went back into Stew's room and closed the door in order to be alone with my Rangers. Actually, I thought I was being considerate because I tend to scream a lot during Rangers games and I didn't want to disturb anyone.

Just the same, you think it might have occurred to me that Stew would be a little unhappy that I had holed myself up in his bedroom to listen to the Rangers game instead of sharing in his birthday festivities. It didn't. Or maybe you're wondering how it must have looked that everyone wanted to spend time with Stew to help him celebrate his birthday . . . except his girlfriend. It hadn't even entered my mind. I was having too much fun, alone on the bed, in Stew's room, with the door closed, listening to the game.

About half an hour later, Stew came in and said, "We're all going over to the Patch for a few drinks. Come on." Now, I noticed he seemed a little upset, but I still had no idea why. Really.

We all walked over to the Patch, which was a corner bar just two houses away. At the bar I could see Stew was definitely pissed off at me. He was completely ignoring me, and he looked like he was trying a little too hard to have a good time. Everyone was buying him shots, and he was kicking them back like they were water. Stew didn't even like to drink shots, and, in situations like this, he and John would usually keep an eye out for each other to make sure neither one did anything really stupid. Not tonight. Every time John told the group that Stew had had enough, Stew would yell something like "Naah! It's my birthday! Give me another shot."

We were at the Patch for no more than an hour and Stew had drunk about six shots, along with a couple of beers. By the time we left, he could barely stand, and his friends had to carry him back to the house. Stew's room was on the first floor and, for some odd reason lost to the history of the house, there was a toilet in the far corner of his room (it was only used in the most desperate circumstances, in case you were wondering). His friends set him down by the toilet, and he started throwing up almost immediately.

I could tell it was going to be a long night, so I went over to check Stew out and see if he wanted water or anything. His head was resting on the toilet, and when I touched his shoulder and asked him how he was doing, he whipped his head around and started yelling at me. I'm not going to tell you what he said, but the gist of it was that he didn't need any help from someone with my family history and that I should do some very bad things to myself and then go home and listen to the end of the Rangers game by myself. Then he turned back to the toilet and threw up again.

Okay, I know I was self-centered, and I *was* wondering what was going on with the Rangers game, but I couldn't just leave Stew like that. Nobody had ever seen him get angry before—only I was capable of making that happen—so when he started yelling at me, everyone else in the house scattered. I just grabbed a blanket off Stew's bed and went off to sleep on the living room couch.

The next morning, when I woke up, Stew was sitting on the couch looking down at me. He felt bad that I had slept on the couch all night, and we started talking about it. Then he remembered why he had been so angry and he started yelling again. I told him I didn't understand why he was so angry and he said, in one breath . . .

"You don't know why I'm angry? I'm with all my friends celebrating my birthday and you're sitting in my room, all by yourself, with the door closed, listening to a [expletive] Rangers game! Then you come out to tell me how excited you are that you can get the Rangers game on the radio and go right back into the room. How's that supposed to make me feel? You'd rather listen to a hockey game by yourself than spend time with me on my birthday! You say I'm your best friend, but what kind of best friend leaves you alone on your birthday!"

To give you the full story, maybe I should tell you what Stew had done for *my* birthday earlier that year. First, he hunted down all of my old friends—the girls from seventh-floor Hart, my hockey teammates, and anyone else he had ever seen me talking with—and told them he was having a surprise birthday party for me at his house and to invite everyone I knew. Then he hitched to the Pen Can Mall in Syracuse to buy me a present (I hated the present—a varnished, two-tiered, ornamental table made out of sliced logs—but it's the thought that counts, right?). Then he took me and a few of my girlfriends out to the Patch while his friends got the party rolling. And then he took me to his house where I was surprised by about a hundred of my friends.

By the end of the party, I had passed out in Stew's room with my contacts in. In 1979 contact lenses were a lot different than they are now and Stew knew if I didn't take mine out, they were going to dry up and I wasn't going to be able to wear them the next day—and he knew that would have been a disaster for me. So he woke me up and forced me to take them out. As you know, I was always having trouble with my contact lenses, but that night it was really bad. No matter what I did, I just couldn't get them out. I was tired of poking myself in the eye and I kept telling Stew that I was just going to sleep with them in. He kept telling me I was going to be really sorry if I didn't take them out. This went on forever, until Stew had another thought. He opened up my contact lens case and saw I had already taken my contacts out and hadn't realized it because I was, how do I say this, too wasted.

You want to know something? Even remembering all this, I still didn't think I had done anything wrong by listening to the Rangers game, and I really couldn't understand why he was so angry. Finally, though, I figured if Stew was that angry, I must have been at least partly to blame and I said I was sorry, which I was. We made up and then sat down for breakfast in the kitchen.

Almost on cue, about five minutes after we stopped yelling, everyone else who lived in the house, and their overnight guests, carefully ventured downstairs to eat breakfast. Once everyone was downstairs, Stew got up and apologized for his behavior. He was really embarrassed. John just looked at him and said, "We didn't hear anything." That was the last anyone ever mentioned of it, and that was when I realized Stew had some really good friends—even if, maybe, I wasn't one of them.

At the end of that year, Stew graduated and I went home for the summer and began an internship at a small Long Island radio station. If you're thinking we broke up once he got out of school, you're wrong. We stayed together and, I think, I began to grow out of some of my selfishness. I'm not saying I changed into the selfless and giving person you know and love today. But I did begin to understand that life would be better for me if I started learning to give instead of always trying to take and keep whatever I could get.

In the fall I applied for, and got, an internship as a field reporter for a radio station in New York, and Stew and I saw each other every weekend. That spring I went back up to Oswego to finish my course work, and Stew said he thought it would be a good idea for us to see other people while I was back up at school. We had our ups and downs, but we made it through and were still together when I graduated at the end of the year.

Nothing else really happened that year, except for my first taste of what it was going to be like as a woman working in a man's world. Even though women were making great strides in the broadcasting business, it was still, for the most part, a good ol' boys' club.

I was working at the radio internship, where I was assigned to work with a well-known street reporter. I was twenty-one and he was fifty, about the same age as Hank was at the time. He was a nice guy, very experienced, and he taught me lot. His wife was also in the business, even more accomplished than he was, and he was nice enough to introduce me to her. It was just a very comfortable situation for me.

One day, about halfway through my internship, I was leaning over my desk, proofing some copy, when this field reporter reached over and, with no warning at all, undid my bra strap. He didn't say anything. He just looked at me and waited for my reaction. I should have slapped him, or worse, but I didn't. I was completely dumbfounded and just stood there. Nothing like that had ever happened to me before and I was totally unprepared to react to it. Finally I turned around and walked over to the bathroom as calmly as I could to put myself back together.

What a valuable experience my internship was. Without it, I might have taken years to realize that accomplished, well-respected married men who introduce you to their wives could still be creeps. Thanks to that internship, I was a little disillusioned, but ready for the real world.

THREE

The Ice Melts Again

After graduating from college, my first career move was to decide whether I should try to get a job in TV or in radio. In the New York area, my on-air TV opportunities were limited to the five local broadcast stations while there were probably about a hundred radio stations, so I picked radio. It really wasn't any more complicated than that.

With all that opportunity, along with my degree in broadcasting, my college radio experience, and two radio internships, I felt I was poised for greatness. I temporarily moved back home with my parents and sent résumés out to every station within commuting distance of my hometown. My efforts were quickly rewarded with my first job out of college. It seems remarkable now, but in less than a month I had landed a position as a cocktail waitress at a local Italian restaurant.

This was going to be harder than I expected—and more humbling. Over the summer, while most of my college friends were finding work in their chosen fields and moving into their own apartments, I was still spending my days looking for a job in my major and my nights at Antonio's, spilling drinks on customers. I could still stop a slap shot heading toward me at 100 mph, but I wasn't able to master the skill set needed to serve drinks with one hand while holding a tray with the other.

The situation at home was no less tumultuous than before I'd gone away to college, and I really couldn't wait to move out on my own. Unfortunately, there was no way I was going to be able to live on my own as long as my main source of income was as a cocktail waitress who couldn't balance a tray of drinks—you don't get much of a tip from someone with a wet lap.

After about four months of trying to get a job in broadcasting, and with no prospects in sight, I came to the realization that I had to try something else. One morning I woke up, drove to the local Taco Bell, and applied for a job. I figured if I could work at Taco Bell during the day and didn't get fired from my night job at Antonio's, I just might make enough money to move into an apartment with a couple of roommates.

Lucky for me, I never got the chance to find out. Later that very same day, as I was getting ready to go to Antonio's, I received a phone call from Frank Brinka, the news director at WALK-AM/FM, a radio station in Patchogue, not far from my home. Frank had listened to my audition tape and wanted me to start right away as a part-time news reporter.

What a break! WALK had a very well-respected news department and one of the most powerful broadcast signals around—I would be heard throughout all of Long Island. As you're reading this, you may be wondering why I settled for a job in news. Well, the reality was that there were no women sports broadcasters that I knew of out there,* and my plans of breaking into sports still seemed to be little more than a dream. Even with my mother telling me I could do anything I wanted,

---

* In actuality, there had been a few women in sports broadcasting before this time, but they were all off my radar for one reason or another: The year before I graduated, Robin Roberts, who was still in college and, later, my colleague at ESPN, had become the sports director for a country music station in Hammond, Louisiana; that same year Mary Carillo served as a tennis analyst for USA Network (analyst jobs are typically filled by former pro athletes); and former beauty queens Phyllis George and Jayne Kennedy had both worked on *NFL Today* in the late '70s.

the idea of ever being a sports broadcaster seemed a remote possibility at best.

As a reporter for WALK, my job was to cover local news events—mainly stories on Suffolk County government and local disasters—all the fun stuff. Usually I'd go out with a tape recorder, conduct a couple of interviews, and then go back to the station and file a report to be played during the hourly newscasts.

I had been working at my new job for only about a week when Frank called me late one night, at home. Uh-oh. I didn't know much about working a paying job at a radio station yet, but I didn't think it was Frank's habit to call reporters at home in the middle of the night to chitchat.

"I just heard the report you filed today that's been on *every* newscast since three o'clock this afternoon. Do you know how many grammatical errors you made in that report?"

The truth was I didn't know I had made any grammatical errors at all. It was lucky for me I was talking to Frank over the phone and not in person. I was flushed and I felt unbearably embarrassed, as if the facade I had now built into that of a bright, perky young college grad with infinite potential had finally been torn away to reveal a stupid, awkward girl who couldn't write to save her life, or her job. I wanted to hang up the phone, run into my room and hide under the covers with that little transistor radio I used to have. But I couldn't hide from something like this.

Frank was really angry. And he was incredulous. He just couldn't believe I could get a four-year degree in communications and not understand the basics of the English language. I figured that was it. I knew if Frank kept putting my reports on the air, he was risking his own reputation and that of the station.

It was clear the easiest and safest thing for Frank to do was fire me. But he didn't. Instead he scheduled a series of meetings between the two of us—actually they were more like lessons—in which we would critique reports written by various members of the news team. He also taught me a straightforward and conversational style of writing that was more appropriate for broadcasting than what I had been using and, at the same time, lessened the likelihood of grammatical errors.

As I mentioned earlier, ever since I was a teenager, a large part of my personal success has been due to men who have had faith in me and were willing to put their own reputations on the line to give me the chance they somehow thought I deserved. Frank Brinka wasn't the last man to do that, but he was probably the most pivotal, because he took what could have been a disastrous situation when I was vulnerable and first starting out in the business and turned it into a learning experience that would give me the writing foundation upon which I would build the rest of my career.

After that, you know, there was no way I was going to let him down. I worked very hard to become the reporter Frank thought I could be. After a while my hard work paid off: He gave me my own news shift to anchor on Sundays.

From there things just kept getting better. As I continued to improve, I was rewarded with a full-time position with more time behind the anchor desk and the opportunity to do a weekly interview piece. One of the first interviews I did was with Buddy McGirt, a young boxer from Brentwood, Long Island, who went on to an amazing career of 73–6–1 with 48 KOs. Although I couldn't get a job in sports broadcasting, I managed to squeeze as much sports into my job as I could get away with.

Even with a job that impressed many of my friends, I was still living at home because my glamorous job as a full-time radio broadcaster left me making no more than half of what most of my college friends were earning. That's just how local radio was. I can only think of one friend, Alison, who was making as little as I was, and she was a social worker. No offense to social workers—they're just horribly underpaid.

But it wasn't the low salary that was bothering me. It was doing news. I guess a lot of people in my position would have looked back on what they had done in such a short time—especially considering my nearly disastrous start—and sat back and savored their accomplishments for a moment.

But that wasn't me. No matter where I've been, or what I've done, I've always wanted more. The prevailing thought in my head has pretty much always been, *Yeah, I've got* [insert whatever I had at the time], *but if I could just get* [insert something I didn't have], *then I would really be happy.* That attitude has certainly wreaked havoc with my personal life, and it's left happiness often just out of reach for me, but it also has been the driving force behind my professional success. Has it been worth it? Maybe by the time I finish writing this book, we'll both know.

So here I was, with a full-time radio job, saying to anyone (other than Frank) who would listen, "Yeah, this is all okay, but if I could just start covering sports, then I would really be happy."

One day I was talking to Doug Geed, the main news anchor and my closest friend at WALK. He and I were always talking about our career goals, and he knew how much I really wanted to be in sports broadcasting. The truth was that everyone at the station knew I was obsessed with sports, and more than one person had made mention of the way I perked up when I did the thirty-second sports segment at the end of my newscast.

Doug said, "You know, WALK carries Islanders games. I bet if you asked Frank, he would let you go down to the Nassau Coliseum and file reports from the game. Tell him you'll do it for free if he pays for your gas."

Doug, who is now at News12 on Long Island, probably doesn't even remember this conversation, but it was the first time I saw the big picture and understood that if I was going to make it into sports broadcasting, I was going to have to put myself in a position to be lucky; to not only hone my skills but also put my talents on display in front of the people who might be interested in hiring me to do sports. The ice had melted for me in college, and I didn't think that kind of luck was likely to occur spontaneously again—but, I thought, if I added a little heat of my own, I might be able to make my own luck.

The catch, of course, was that I had to cover the Islanders, the nemesis of every Rangers fan alive, and certainly my own personal sworn enemy. It was a cruel fate for someone like me, but I knew I had to make sacrifices if I was ever going to make it into sports broadcasting. This was a big sacrifice, though, because I had to change my behavior as well as my objectivity.

See what I mean: One of the first games I covered for WALK was an Islanders–Rangers playoff. It was overtime, and the score was tied. When Don Maloney scored the tying goal with one minute left to send the game into overtime, I jumped out of my seat in the press box and started screaming just as I would at any Rangers game—that is, until I noticed all my colleagues were still sitting there, fully composed, doing their jobs and looking at me. *Oh,* I thought, *I guess it's not cool to root against the team you're covering.* Of course, part of me also thought, *What? Just because I'm covering the game I can't enjoy it?* But after that I learned to sit on my hands and keep my mouth shut, at least most of the time. (The Rangers, as was their habit back then, went on to lose in overtime on a Ken Morrow goal from the point that got by a screened Glen Hanlon.)

Another big sacrifice I had to make to cover the Islanders was to walk into the locker room after each game to interview the players. To make things perfectly clear, let me emphasize that the only reason a female reporter wants to get into the locker room after a game is for equal access to the players. There's no comparison between the quality of an interview gotten right after a game and one that's done half an hour later after the players have showered, settled down, and gotten into their street clothes. I think I speak for 99 percent of all the female reporters who have ever traversed a male locker room when I say that there is absolutely nothing sexy, stimulating, or the least bit enticing for a female reporter when she walks into a men's locker room.

First of all, sweaty, tired, half-naked men walking around a damp locker room strewn with smelly and, sometimes, blood-soaked jerseys and undergarments is anything but sexy. Second, a woman reporter usually makes such a tremendous effort to make sure she doesn't give even the impression that she's looking anywhere but where she is supposed to be looking, that it becomes difficult to develop a natural and relaxed interviewing rapport with the athlete.

The real challenge, though, is when a hockey player comes up to you to do an interview and then drops his towel just as you're about to ask your first question. Once again, for the guys, because I know it's difficult for you to understand, just because it may be a fantasy of yours for a woman to come up to you in a locker room somewhere and drop her towel, the opposite does not hold true. It really doesn't. In fact, it's a little creepy.

And while I'm clarifying things, let me say that in no way did I ever consider a male athlete taking off his towel in front of me to be an act of aggression or sexual harassment. Sure, I wish they all could have just kept themselves covered up, but I understood that I was in a men's locker room and that, when it's 1982, and you're in a men's locker room and you're not a man, you have to expect some commotion.

I knew, by going into the locker room, that I was creating a situation only a little less awkward for the players than it was for me, and rather than taking offense, I had to understand that their pranks were just a harmless attempt to relieve the tension. Sure, I knew I was the butt of their joke (no pun intended), but I also knew that if I was going to go into the men's locker room, I had to be able to take a joke. So I did.

On the other hand, before the politically correct police get all up in arms and tell me I've taken women's rights in the work-place back fifty years, let me give you an example of what I do think harassment is:

A few years after the falling-towel incident, I went into a locker room at a Mets game to interview one of the stars of the game, an infielder. The Mets had won and he should have been in a good mood, but as soon as I introduced myself he started lashing into me. First, he said I was a &@#$!; then he told me that a &@#$! had no business being in a men's locker room and that I should get the !&*$# out.

Now, *that* was harassment.

That wasn't the first or last time I had been sexually harassed while doing my job, but I think that's enough about that subject for now. Let's get back to the Islanders. Do you know how they say it's difficult to hate someone once you get to know them? Well, that hasn't always been my experience, but it was definitely the case for me when I got to know the Islanders, and that really messed with my sense of the world order and team loyalty. How do you reconcile liking a team you know you were born to hate? Then again, if I could learn to like the Islanders, maybe there was a chance for world peace.

Here's how it happened. The Islanders were the only professional sports team on Long Island and, perhaps because of that, relations between the players, the fans, and the press were marked by mutual appreciation and camaraderie. After every home game members of all three groups would head down the road to Dr. Generosity's, a nearby watering hole, to celebrate the win or commiserate the loss. There wasn't any trash talking among the fans or elitism among the team members. We felt like we were all in it together. As a result, I got to know the Islanders pretty well on and off the ice and, even though I couldn't ever bring myself to root for them, I came to admire and appreciate them, as a team and as individuals. They were the perfect first team for a sports reporter to cover.

As luck would have it, they were also the perfect team to cover for someone who was always looking for something better in her career. Since the Islanders were in the midst of their four–Stanley Cup dynasty, they were receiving a good amount of attention beyond their regular fan base. As a result, high-level

New York broadcasters who wouldn't ordinarily venture past the borders of New York City were heading out to Uniondale, Long Island, to cover the Islanders.

One of those people was Ed Ingles, the heralded sports director for WCBS Newsradio 88, who, for about a year before I met him, had been looking to add a woman sportscaster to his staff. At the time, Newsradio was the consummate source for the most up-to-date sports (and news) in the city. In the early 1980s there was no such thing as the Internet or all-sports radio; even ESPN was still just emerging as the sports powerhouse it would later become. If someone wanted up-to-date sports information, the place most people went was to Newsradio.

After observing my coverage of the Islanders for a while, Ed asked me if I would be interested in working for CBS, filing reports for the Mets and US Open tennis. It wasn't anything more than a freelance position, but for me it was the first time I was actually getting paid to be a sports reporter. I jumped at the opportunity.

When I started writing this book, I asked Ed why, after spending a year looking for a woman, he ended up hiring me. He said, "Linda, I saw in you what I saw in myself, someone who knew and loved sports and was going to work harder than anyone else. Then, when I hired you, I saw that you didn't give up no matter what, you just tried to get better. Everyone makes mistakes, but the good ones remember their mistakes."

This was another turning point in my career, because it made me the first woman ever to be heard delivering dedicated sports coverage on a New York City radio station. Just as importantly, the fact that Ed Ingles, one of the most respected men in New York sports broadcasting, was willing to take a chance and hire me as the first woman to work at CBS's flagship radio station gave me an unmatched level of credibility.

CBS was in Manhattan and about a two-hour commute from Coram, Long Island, where I was still living with my parents. To cut my commute in half, I started staying overnight in Plainview a lot, where Stew lived with his parents.

So, you might wonder, how were things going between me and Stew? Well, really pretty well, although there were times when I definitely tested his patience and gave him mixed messages. For example, about a year after I got out of school I almost broke up with him so I could start seeing a reporter who was also working the Islanders games. Then, six months later, I sort of tried to force him to propose, even though I didn't want to get married (it was my mother's idea).

The truth was, growing up the way I had, I just wasn't aptly prepared to be in a loving and selfless relationship. Here's what I mean:

Shortly after I started working at CBS, Stew and I took the train together into New York one morning and then headed off to our respective jobs. Later that morning he sent a dozen long-stemmed red roses to my office. As soon as they came, I called him on the phone, and here's how the conversation went:

Me: Hi. It's me.
Stew: Hey, Lin. How's it going?
Me: I got the flowers you sent.
Stew: Do you like them?
Me: What's wrong?
Stew: What do you mean?

Me: I mean, you sent me a dozen red roses and it's not my birthday or anything. Something must be wrong.

Stew: Nothing's wrong. I just was thinking about you and felt like sending you some flowers.

Me: Really?

Stew: Really.

Me: I don't understand.

Stew: Well, I guess I never really thought about it, but if there was something wrong, or if I did something wrong, I wouldn't send you flowers, I would sit down and talk to you about it. If I'm sending you flowers, it's because I'm happy and I want to help brighten up your day a little. Okay?

Me: Okay.

Stew: I gotta go. I'll talk to you later.

Me: Okay. Luv ya!

Stew: Yeah, me too. Bye.

Even though I couldn't see him, I was pretty sure Stew was shaking his head in disbelief as he hung up. After that, he didn't send me flowers again for a long time. With negative feedback like that from me, why would he?

That conversation seems ridiculous to me now, but I had never before been in a relationship of any kind in which someone did something nice for me without expecting anything in return. At least I hadn't noticed it. It always seemed that in my world, if someone did something nice for you, it was either because they felt guilty, they wanted something from you, or they wanted to make themselves look good. This was going to take some getting used to.

Over the next few months, I continued to place myself in a position to be lucky. Ed gave me a regular, overnight-weekend shift and, because of my exposure on Newsradio, I became aware of, and was offered, the weekend-afternoon news shift at CBS-FM, the New York oldies station.

Back then "oldies" meant music from the 1950s, '60s, and early '70s, and all the DJs I had grown up with listening to WABC on my little transistor radio—Harry Harrison, Cousin Brucie, and Ron Lundy, to name a few—had transplanted themselves to CBS-FM. If I couldn't get more sports work, the next best thing was for me to be working with all those great DJs while listening to the music of my childhood (well, not the '50s stuff, but the '60s and '70s for sure).

To my surprise, WALK considered CBS-FM to be a direct competitor and said I couldn't work at both stations. CBS-FM was offering me $200 a week just to work the weekends for them. It wasn't a lot of money, but it was pretty good for working just two days a week, and it was more than I was making working five days for WALK, so I said good-bye to Frank Brinka, Doug Geed, and WALK, and never looked back.

Now I had two weekend jobs—Newsradio and CBS-FM—but nothing to do during the week. To fill up the time, I got a regular news job at WGBB, another Long Island radio station with a news department even bigger than WALK's. They took their news so seriously that they had two, instead of one, newscasts an hour as well as their own traffic plane—okay, not as prestigious as the traffic helicopter at Newsradio, but pretty cool for Long Island.

Around the same time, Stew and I moved into a little apartment in Briarwood, a small section of Queens between Kew Gardens and Jamaica. I was now working three jobs, seven days a week, so I didn't spend much time at the apartment, but I do remember that the building we lived in was infested with roaches and it utterly grossed me out. I hate bugs of all kinds, but roaches are definitely among the most abhorrent in my mind.

Things at CBS, both at Newsradio and CBS-FM, were working out well, and I was getting a lot of positive feedback. I thought, since I had been able to leverage my experience at CBS to get a position with CBS-FM, I might be able to leverage my experience at both radio stations to get some work at CBS-TV. I knew it was a long shot, but you never know unless you try.

Ted Shaker was the sports director for all of CBS-TV and, as a CBS employee, I was able to just call his office and ask for an appointment with him. It became clear pretty early into our meeting that Ted wasn't going to be making me any offers that day, but he was very nice and very patient. He was familiar with my work on CBS Radio and encouraged me to keep up the good work. We talked sports for a while and, as our meeting was coming to an end, he asked if there was anything he could do for me. I thought about just coming right out and asking him for a job, but I knew, given the circumstances, that it would seem absurd. Instead I asked him if he had any advice for me in terms of improving my performance or furthering my career.

He said, "Just be accurate. Don't worry about anything else. Because you're a woman, listeners will be waiting for you to make a mistake so they can dismiss you. They want to be able to say you don't know anything about sports because you're a woman. But if you're accurate, no one can have anything on you."

That advice is as true and valuable to me today as it was back then. Even twenty years later there are still viewers out there just waiting for me to make a mistake so they can pounce. And this is another place where I think I need to clarify my position a little so that I'm not misunderstood.

If I make a mistake and someone calls me on it, I appreciate the correction and accept the honest criticism. If viewers leave their phone number or e-mail address, I'll usually get back to them and thank them. Even though I strive for perfection, almost everything I do is live and under pressure; sometimes I'm going to make a mistake and I don't want to make the same mistake twice, so I welcome the call.

If viewers send me an e-mail because they disagree with my point of view, that's even better. I love a good sports debate, and the only thing I enjoy more than mixing it up with a real sports fan with a legitimate point of view is when that sports fan is ten years old. Honestly, there's nothing better than sharing in the pure, unadulterated joy of a ten-year-old sports fan talking to you about his or her favorite team.

On the other hand, if I get a profanity-laced voice mail at work from someone who tells me I'm incompetent or worse because I mispronounced the name of a new Czech hockey player in his first NHL appearance, I don't even get halfway through the message before I skip to the next one. I don't have time for people who try to make themselves feel better by putting other people down.

Back at WGBB I was crazy busy all the time because I had to get a newscast ready every half hour and because they wanted me to jam as much information into each newscast as possible. I had so much writing to do that I was assigned a college intern to help me put together my newscast. Most college interns, even the ones with good writing skills, don't have the practical experience necessary to understand what to include in a news piece and what not to, but the kid they assigned to me was different. He knew his way around a newsroom and could write a piece with almost no input from me. Something was going on with him, and I wanted to know what it was.

After he had been helping me out for a few days, I said to him, "Hey, kid, how come you aren't just getting me a bagel and coffee like the other interns. Where'd you learn to write like that? What's your story?"

It turned out this kid was a senior at the New York Institute of Technology where they had a daily cable television news show; he was a reporter for that show. It was an unbelievable opportunity for a college student, or anyone looking to get into TV. He told me about his experience and then said "If you're interested, why don't you shadow me on a story sometime?"

It was kind of presumptuous for a college intern to ask a "professional" newscaster like me to help him out on his internship, *for free,* just because I expressed some interest in what he was doing. Someone else might have thought the offer was demeaning, and I know some of my colleagues did when they heard about it. But I didn't see it that way. I knew the kid was just trying to help out someone he saw as a colleague, so I took the opportunity and became my intern's intern.

This "kid," by the way was Brian Kenny, and, it seemed that our paths were destined to cross over and over again. Brian eventually moved up to serve as chief correspondent, where he anchored the news, did feature stories, and oversaw the other reporters. I kept doing free intern work and helping out wherever I was needed, but I wasn't able to do any on-air work.

When Brian graduated from New York Tech, he was hired at WLIG-55, another cable station, where he eventually became the sports anchor. He had the job I wanted! But his leaving *LI News Tonight* opened up a spot for a new chief correspondent at New York Tech, and I talked the management over there into letting me audition.

I had never done a newscast in front of a TV camera before and I was a little nervous, but I figured I had nothing to lose and I relied on my radio experience to pull me through. I think to almost everyone's surprise, I did pretty well—well enough, anyway—and they hired me at the whopping salary of $100 a week (previously, the job had always gone to an unpaid student intern, so I was happy to get the hundred bucks). That was my big break into TV and, as chief correspondent, I had my hands in everything. Everything, that is, except for sports. Even though I had been reporting sports on the radio for three years and was, at the time, doing it for the prestigious Newsradio 88, New York Tech still thought it was too risky to put a woman sportscaster on TV.

So now I was working four jobs. I was a news anchor at WGBB weekday mornings, chief correspondent for *LI News Tonight* weekday evenings, news anchor for WCBS-FM weekend afternoons, and I filed overnight sports reports for Newsradio 88 on weekend nights. In my free time, I ended up getting married. Yes, it was Stew I married, and even though I cried on our way over to the courthouse to get the marriage license, our future seemed bright. Really. Well, sort of anyway.

FOUR

Marital Bliss

A couple of weeks before Stew and I got married, I left WGBB. Working four jobs had gotten to be too much; I needed a break. It wasn't long after returning from our honeymoon, though, that I added another job, or two, or three . . . thanks, in part, to Brian Kenny.

Brian was now the sports anchor at Channel 55, and when they assigned him to cover the US Golf Open being held on Long Island at the Shinecock Hills Golf Club, he asked his news director if he could hire a couple of reporters to help him out. One of the reporters he hired was me. My job was to do feature and sidebar reports.

When the Open was over, Channel 55 liked me well enough to keep me on as a part-time reporter. In addition to my work at Channel 55 I started working as a part-time news anchor under the pseudonym of Carol Stewart at WNSR, a soft rock station in Manhattan. Unlike WALK, CBS allowed me to work at WNSR as long as I used a different name. Carol was my middle name and Stewart was, well, you know.

Shortly after I landed that job, I also began as a part-time news reporter for News 12 Long Island (another Long Island cable TV station) and, in my free time, I picked up some stringing work—that is, freelance sports reporting.

Stew and I were still sharing our apartment with an extended family of roaches, but it hardly mattered because I was hardly there. Stew was hardly there either: He was working in the marketing research department of a small advertising agency during the day and going to graduate school at night.

On the weekends I was working midday at CBS-FM and overnight at Newsradio. The only social life we had was going out after work for a couple of hours with our respective coworkers. As for time together, that was limited pretty much to Friday nights—the one night of the week I didn't work—when we would usually sit together in front of the TV with a couple of glasses of milk and a big bag of M&M's until, despite all the sugar coursing through our veins, we couldn't keep our eyes open anymore and went to bed.

Other than those brief interludes on Friday nights, I was spending most of what little free time I had seeking out bigger and better job opportunities. What was I looking for? Anything different from what I was already doing looked attractive, even if it didn't make much sense from a long-term career perspective. For instance, as a result of the exposure I was getting at CBS, I received a call from Shadow Traffic—a syndicated traffic news service—to work as a full-time traffic reporter. Even though reporting traffic during morning and afternoon drive times had absolutely nothing to do with what I liked or wanted to do, I seriously considered taking the job because it would put me on almost every major radio station in New York and offered me a full-time paycheck.

Ultimately, I decided not to take the job, as much because it was a split shift (6:00 to 10:00 a.m., then 3:00 to 7:00 p.m.) and too long a commute (to New Jersey) as because it had nothing to do with sports, but it's surprising how close I actually got to accepting a job that might have derailed my career in sports broadcasting.

Another opportunity I had to think long and hard about was Sportsphone. This was a new concept developed in the mid-1980s where a customer would dial a premium-priced, 976 phone number and, in fifty-eight seconds, get an update on everything that was going on in sports around the country. As with Shadow Traffic, my exposure on Newsradio prompted them to recruit me. I didn't have to do anything to get the job except say yes.

Sportsphone was like nothing I had ever done before. I worked the weekday night shift and spent my time there in a small room with dingy white walls, five TVs hooked up to cable, and a sports ticker. I usually shared the room with three or four guys who were doing reports for other parts of the country and, because I was in the minority, one of the TVs was almost always tuned to the Playboy Channel—I got used to it. I had no choice, but it was no big deal.

My Sportsphone report had to be updated every ten minutes. For eight and a half minutes, I watched games on four of the TVs, read the sports ticker, debated sports issues with my coworkers, and wrote, and rewrote, my report. With about fifteen seconds to go, I would walk into a tiny booth that had only a telephone, a microphone, and a countdown timer. For soundproofing, they had put up cheap, crumbly, cork wall tiles you could buy at Woolworth for a couple of bucks a package. It made one of those study rooms in the Oswego Library look like a luxury hotel suite.

Once I closed the not-very-soundproof door behind me, I picked up the phone and dialed a number that patched me into the New York Sportsphone feed. Through the telephone earpiece came this eerie, monotonous tone. When the tone stopped, it was the signal for me to begin. I started the countdown timer and read my report into the microphone. After exactly fifty-eight seconds, the eerie tone would abruptly come back on and cut off my microphone. If I didn't finish my report before the tone came back on, or if I made a mistake during my report, it didn't matter. Whatever I said, or didn't say, in those fifty-eight seconds was what sports fans in the New York area heard when they called in for the next ten minutes.

It sounds like grueling work, but it was fun and gave me invaluable experience. First, it forced me to learn to write for time and under tremendous pressure, making writing under any other circumstances seem relatively easy. Second, I got to spend my nights talking sports with a bunch of guys who were as passionate about the subject as I was.

When Sportsphone offered me a full-time position, I had another difficult decision to make. I still wanted the security of a full-time position, but I wasn't sure I wanted to give up my exposure on radio and TV. I was afraid I would be forgotten—both by listeners/viewers and by the broadcast profession—if I was only heard over a telephone. Sportsphone seemed like a great concept, but I wasn't sure if fifty-eight-second sports reports over the telephone were really going to be the wave of the future. In the end I decided to leave Sportsphone and continue my pursuits in radio and TV. Considering that Sportsphone folded soon after, I think I made the right move.

As it turns out, another new opportunity was about to open up for me when Brian Kenny left Channel 55 to become the sports director at WTZA-TV in Kingston, New York. I had been reporting for Channel 55 for some time and, when Brian left, they were familiar enough with my work to let me anchor the sports desk without even an audition. It was a bad move on their part.

Shortly after I started as sports anchor, Brian was talking to Danny Guido, a good friend of his and my cameraman on the show. During the course of their conversation, he asked how I was doing in my new role. Danny said, "Oh, buddy, it's really bad. I'm sure she's going to get better, but right now it's a disaster."

Yeah, I still had some work to do. I'm not sure why I was so much worse as a sports anchor at Channel 55 than I'd been as a news anchor at *LI News Tonight*. It might have been that, as a sports anchor for Channel 55, I was also the producer. It was cool to have my name listed in the credits as a producer, but I had never acted as a TV producer before and my radio experience didn't translate very well into video production.

Still, the benefit of working for a local cable station back then was that they had a lot of patience and the viewer base was localized, so my exposure to the outside world was limited. Over time, I did get better, but I had to leave Channel 55 long before I showed any inkling of being ready for ESPN. The commute from my apartment in Queens to the station, out on eastern Long Island, was way too long, and it was dragging on me.

Back in Manhattan, a full-time news anchor position opened up at WNSR, the soft-rock music station I had been working for part-time. It wasn't sports, but it was a full-time position at a Manhattan-based radio station. I wanted it. At least I thought I did.

NSR was considering only two people for the position, me and the future Deborah Rodriguez. Debbie, who is now a long-time anchor at Newsradio, had been a friend and colleague at WGBB and, like me, had been working at NSR as a part-time news anchor. If I remember correctly, she actually helped me get my part-time position at NSR. I liked Debbie, but my competitive nature overcame me and I not only wanted to get the job, but I wanted to beat out Debbie. It wasn't anything personal; I just wanted, as usual, to win.

In the end Debbie "won," although I expect she wasn't warped enough to think of it in quite that way. I remember that sunken feeling in my chest when Ted David,* the news director, called me into his office to tell me I hadn't gotten the job. When he was done, I just wanted to get out of his office and call Stew to tell him the bad news. But then I realized that Ted hadn't stopped talking; he was just changing the subject. He told me one of the reasons he didn't give me the news anchor job was because he didn't think I should be doing news. He said I should be concentrating on sports because that was where my passion lay.

Then he told me he knew Shelby Whitfield, the director for ABC Radio Sports. He picked up the phone right then and there, called Shelby, and handed me the phone. Shelby knew of me and invited me to his office to talk.

When I met with him, we talked for a little while and then, on the spot, he offered me a job doing sports for the WABC Entertainment Network. This was the most exciting job offer I had received since I first got that call from Frank Brinka.

---

* Ted is currently the senior anchor for CNBC Business Radio and does occasional anchoring for News 12 Long Island.

Working for the ABC Entertainment Network, I would be heard at hundreds of radio stations across the country, although not in New York, and I only had to do one two-minute newscast at 6:00 a.m. and another at 4:20 p.m. It was a split shift, but it was a full-time sports job with full-time pay, and I was going to be heard all around the country. The bonus was that ABC had the broadcast rights to the upcoming Olympics, and they would be sending me to Calgary and Seoul. I accepted the job the next day.

When I told my bosses at Newsradio that I was leaving, they were a little upset that I hadn't spoken to them before I accepted the offer at ABC. They didn't want to lose me and said they were going to come back with a counteroffer. I felt awful that I hadn't spoken to them sooner—CBS had been very good to me—but it had never occurred to me that they would be willing to offer me a full-time position. I told them I would consider their counteroffer, which they needed some time to put together.

In the meantime I was having a different type of problem at CBS: I was receiving threatening letters through the mail. Ironically, when I began at CBS as the first woman sportscaster to be heard in New York, I didn't generate any negative feedback from listeners. Over time I even developed a small fan base, and once a week the mailroom would send up a small pile of positive fan mail, but it wasn't until I was planning to leave CBS that I started getting hate mail—and the mail I was receiving was really hateful.

All the mail came from the same sender and started off the same way. The return address on the envelope always listed the name and internal business address of a CBS executive—the name was different on each envelope—making me want to open it right away. Inside was a typewritten letter telling me how much the writer hated me and promising that he was going to abduct me and perform horrible, sexually sadistic acts upon me, most of which would have ended up with me dead, or at least horribly maimed.

Honestly, I was really frightened. CBS security got involved, but they were unable to develop any leads. The letters weren't being mailed from within CBS, although the writer was obviously someone familiar with the company's organization. The only peace of mind they could give me was to tell me that, usually, people who wrote threatening letters like this were not the type to actually do anything. I solved the problem by handing over any new suspicious mail I received to Stew so he could check it over before I looked at it. If it wasn't a legitimate letter, he would just rip it up.

It was at that time, though, that I came to terms with the fact that as long as I was in the public eye, I was going to get threatening and hateful mail from people who had too much time on their hands. I've long since stopped reading letters like that. As soon as realize I'm reading one of those letters, I fold it up, put it back in the envelope, and lock it up in a drawer for safekeeping, just in case. As my ESPN colleague Chris Fowler once said to me, "If they find you at the bottom of a ditch somewhere, maybe the letters will help them find the guy." Not exactly a pleasant thought, but if I'm going to be brutally murdered by a perverse lunatic, at least I can take my last breath knowing that some CSI agent will be hard at work, examining those letters for evidence.

While I was still coming to terms with the threatening letters, CBS came back to me with an offer higher than ABC's. Now I was really torn. I had a lot of loyalty to CBS because they had given me my big break and made me feel like a member of the CBS family, even when I was just working freelance. On the other hand, I had accepted the job at ABC and I felt my word was as good as a written contract. In my business, and in life, I believe that if you don't stand by your word, then you don't have anything. Still, I felt that, no matter what decision I made, I would be doing something wrong to somebody.

I eventually went back to Shelby and told him about the situation I was in. He understood and told me he'd get back to me. After a few days, he came back with an offer substantially higher than the one from CBS, which prompted CBS to tell me I had received an offer I couldn't refuse and, in effect, give me their blessing to go to ABC. That's how I became the first woman sportscaster to work for a national radio network.

After accepting the job at ABC, I had to let go of my part-time work at Newsradio, CBS-FM, and WNSR, because they were all considered direct competitors. I was allowed to continue my part-time work at *LI News Tonight,* however, and I got to fill in for Charlie Steiner, another future ESPN colleague, at WABC radio in New York.

With my full-time job at ABC and Stew with a new job at an established marketing research company, we felt financially secure enough to move to a bigger apartment. After searching for a long time, we found a nice place on the first floor of a two-family house in the Ditmars Boulevard section of Astoria, Queens. The streets of this neighborhood were lined with old brick homes, and the owners of these homes usually lived in one of the apartments. In the house we lived in, our landlord, Ralph, lived upstairs with his two young children. They were a nice family, and we felt lucky to be able to move into an area with such a neighborhood feel. Personally, I was overjoyed to move into a place without roaches.

It seemed, however, that the neighborhood wasn't quite as happy to have us as we were to be a part of it. We moved into our new apartment in early summer and were eager to get an air conditioner into our bedroom window, both so we could beat the heat at night and drown out the street noise.

I was inside the bedroom holding down the window so our just-bought air conditioner wouldn't fall to the pavement while Stew went outside with a stepladder to secure it. Stew was outside for just a few minutes when he met our new next-door neighbor, Julio, a first-generation Italian gentleman in his forties:

Julio: Hey, what are you doing?

Stew: I'm putting in an air conditioner.

Julio: Did you get permission to put it in?

Stew: Yeah, I asked Ralph and he said it was okay.

Julio: That air conditioner is hanging over my driveway. It's not Ralph you have to get permission from. It's me.

Stew: Okay. Is it all right if I put in the air conditioner?

Julio: Does it drip? I don't want it dripping water on my driveway.

Stew: I don't know. It's a new air conditioner. I've never used it before.

Julio: You can't put it in if it drips. It will crack my concrete. Does it drip?

Stew: Well, I don't know because I've never used it before. It's brand new, but if it drips, there's an attachment for a hose and I can route the water into a small bucket so it won't drip on the driveway.

Julio: All right, but I don't want it falling out of the window onto my car. I park my car under that window sometimes.

Stew: Don't worry. I've put in air conditioners before. I'll make sure it's secure in the window.

Julio: Okay, I'll let you put it in, but if there are any problems, you're going to have to take it out.

Stew: Okay. You just let me know.

I was fuming! What was this guy's problem? It was only an air conditioner and, besides, there was no way I was going to endure even one summer in Astoria without an air conditioner, whether it leaked water or not. What did the guy do about his precious concrete when it rained?

When Stew came back into the apartment, I told him I wanted to go next door and give Julio a piece of my mind, but Stew didn't want us to get off on the wrong foot. He said I had to try to see it from Julio's point of view. We were the new neighbors, and Julio was just trying to protect himself from strangers. He said that we'd probably find out he was a nice guy once we all got to know each other.

The very next day we got to find out whether Stew was right or not. Julio met him on the sidewalk and said, "Another thing, make sure your wife doesn't park in front of my driveway. I go to work early in the morning and I don't want to be blocked in."

What was he talking about? So much for the nice guy next door. Nonetheless, Stew was insistent that we do our best not to ruffle any feathers in our new neighborhood. Besides, he reasoned, what was the difference? We never would have parked in front of Julio's driveway anyway. It was against the law. Who does that in New York?

Anyway, I knew I had to listen to Stew because I was the one in our relationship who usually lost patience and created a problem with people we were going to have to get along with. Stew was the one who would come over after I screwed everything up to smooth things out. As much as I didn't like to admit it, he had gotten me out of a few sticky jams in the past, most recently when I'd opened my mouth a little too wide at a sports bar filled with Islanders fans and called one of them a bad name loud enough for them to hear.

After a few more weeks, though, it turned out that Stew had been right about Julio after all. Before our second month's rent was due, Julio once again stopped Stew on the street.

"Look, I don't like Linda parking on the street. It's still dark when she goes to work in the morning and it's not safe for a young woman like her to be on the street at that time. You tell her I want her to park the car overnight in my driveway so she doesn't have to walk in the street. She leaves for work before I do, so it won't be a problem. Tell her I insist."

After that, we never had another problem in the neighborhood, and Julio was always looking out for us. I wouldn't say we became good friends—just good neighbors, which in some ways are more valuable. When the battery in our Civic died, Julio was out there with Stew, helping him put a new one in; and if Julio had a new project going on in his basement workshop, he would invite Stew over to take a look at it and share a drink or two of the exotic liqueur in the long, stretched-out bottle he kept there just for such occasions.

A couple of years later, when we left Astoria, Julio gave us a small religious keepsake he had gotten when he visited the Vatican: something to remember him by and to bring us good Grace. For me, it was a reminder of how first impressions can be wrong and that a little patience and understanding can completely change the nature of a relationship.

The funny thing about working for the ABC Entertainment Network was that I was heard in large and small markets throughout the country, but not at all in New York, where I worked. The benefit was that, because I was not heard in New York, ABC let me do freelance work on WFAN, the world's first 24/7 sports talk station. By the way, the FAN, as they call it, has always been a friendly place for women sportscasters. The first voice ever heard on WFAN was that of Suzyn Waldman as she gave the station's first sports update at 3:00 p.m. on July 1, 1987.

My first job at WFAN was as a fill-in for those two-minute sports updates that aired three times every hour. After a few months Len Weiner, the sport director, asked me if I was interested in doing a Sunday brunch interview/call-in show at Rusty Staub's restaurant on Fifth Avenue in Manhattan.

Just in case you're not a hard-core Mets fan like I am, let me tell you that Rusty Staub was a Mets star in the early 1970s and then again in the early '80s. Among other things, he was a big reason the Mets upset the Reds in the 1973 National League Championship Series; in 1983 he also tied the record for the most RBI by a pinch hitter. I was a huge fan and I was thrilled to be making my call-in show debut at his restaurant. I also thought it would be fun to do a show in front of a live audience while they were sipping Bloody Marys and Mimosas on Sunday mornings.

For my first show, I was scheduled to interview Evander Holyfield, the future heavyweight champion of the world. I had been following Evander's career ever since the 1984 Summer Olympics, but I felt I was nowhere near knowledgeable enough to spend two hours talking to him and taking calls about his career. I spent all my free time the week before the interview studying up and taking notes in preparation for my very first show.

When I walked into the restaurant the day of the show with twenty pages of handwritten notes, my producer almost had a heart attack. He said there was no way I was going to be able to rely on notes to do a call-in show. He'd never seen anyone do it like that before, and it just didn't work that way. I think he would have canceled the show if he could have, but I told him I knew what I was doing and that everything was going to be fine.

It was the first call-in show I had ever done so, of course, I had no idea whether it was going to be fine or not. The only thing I did know was that I had done everything I possibly could to get ready. Except now that I saw how nervous my producer was, I was getting worried that I might blow the whole thing.

Stew was at a nearby table with a group of his friends who were all there to watch my debut at Rusty's—not too much pressure. I pulled him aside and told him what my producer had said to me. By this time I didn't know what was right anymore, and I was thinking of ditching my notes completely. Stew said what he's always said to me in times like this: "You're going to be fine. You've prepared the best way you know how. Just be yourself, go out there, and do it."

As it turns out, everything was fine. Evander was a kind, thoughtful, and intelligent interview, and I was able to interact with the fans who called in without any trouble. By the end of the two hours, my twenty pages of notes were strewn all over the table, but I had emerged from my first show unscathed, and FAN wanted me to do it all over again the following week.

Over time I learned to rely less on my notes and more on my instinct. I started having more fun with my guests and callers, and I felt I was starting to get into a groove. After each show a few restaurant patrons would come up to me to talk sports or ask me for an autograph. I felt like a real celebrity.

The only thing gnawing at me was that I never heard from Rusty. I hadn't been the first one from the FAN to do a show at his restaurant, and I had heard that he often called in after a show to thank the host and talk for a few minutes. I was getting good feedback from my producer, but I still needed that phone call from Rusty to validate me.

About the third or fourth time I did the show, that call finally came in. We were taking a commercial break about an hour into the broadcast when my producer came up to me and said, "Rusty just called."

I was elated. This is what I had been waiting for. With anticipation, I asked, "What did he say?"

"He said to tell you that the name of his restaurant is *Rusty's on Fifth,* not *Rusty's,* and to make sure you say *Rusty's on Fifth* when you promote the restaurant during the show. Rusty's is a different restaurant he owns downtown and he doesn't want them confused."

"That's all he said?"

"That's it."

That was the first and last time I ever heard from Rusty. I guess he wasn't as big a fan of Linda Cohn as I was of him. A couple of weeks after that phone call, I stopped doing shows from the restaurant. That was okay. For some reason my heart wasn't in it anymore anyway. Besides, I had to start preparing for my trip to Calgary and the Winter Olympics!

Being in Calgary was like living in a three-week-long dream sequence. To begin with, I loved anything and everything about Canada because it was the birthplace of modern hockey and the NHL, my first love. When I got there I also loved that Calgary combined the ruggedness of the Old West—cowboys, rodeos, and great steaks—with a lively, cosmopolitan city that still, somehow, felt small and friendly. I think what I loved most, though, was that, because ABC had the broadcast rights to the Olympics, I could go and do whatever I wanted, whenever I wanted. All I needed was to show my press pass and I was treated like royalty.

I was having such a great time that I didn't want it to end. I mean, I *really* didn't want it to end. I liked living a life of privilege in a fun city where everyone seemed different and exciting, and I wasn't looking forward to going back to Astoria, my split shift at the studio, or Stew. It all seemed so boring.

Getting on the plane to go back to New York was a real letdown, and sitting in the plane for five hours gave me a lot of time to think about things. By the time we landed at JFK Airport, I was totally confused and questioning everything about my life.

Stew was waiting for me at the airport with a big smile on his face. To me, everything just seemed strange and uncomfortable. He was wearing a bold red-and-black sweater that was very different from the casual jeans and sweatshirt he usually had on, and he seemed unfamiliar to me. I felt like I didn't know who he was.

"Why are you wearing that sweater?" I asked.

"You gave it to me before you left as a present. Remember?" He was still smiling.

"Oh. You seem weird. Different somehow."

That took the smile off his face all right.

In the car home, the conversation escalated.

"What are you talking about?" he said. "We've been together for ten years. We've been living together for over three years, you're away for three weeks and you think I'm different? I don't know what you're talking about!"

I didn't know what I was talking about either, but everything seemed so weird. I hadn't seen Stew for three weeks and didn't even care. Something was wrong. I didn't know what it all meant and I was afraid to find out.

I buried those feelings and went back to my life in Astoria. Within a few weeks Calgary was just a fond memory, and everything between Stew and I seemed back to normal.

I may have been confused about my personal life, but my career goals were becoming very clear. For the last few years, my sights had been targeted on constantly gaining more experience and improving my marketability, whether it meant working in radio or TV or even Sportsphone. Now I knew I wanted to make a dedicated commitment to getting a full-time job in TV.

It wasn't that I didn't like radio anymore. Both TV and radio have their appeal to me. With radio, there's an intimacy between broadcaster and listener that I don't think gets through on television. TV, in comparison, gives you more tools to communicate with and allows you to get right into the viewer's living room. What made me choose TV, I think, was that it was a much more competitive field, and I couldn't walk away from the competition. I had to see if I could make it.

I also knew exactly where I wanted to work—Calgary. By now, you must be beginning to understand that I loved the novelty of anything new. A few years earlier, Stew and I had gone on a two-week-long vacation to California—it was the first time either one of us had been west of New Jersey—and I fell so in love with it that I wanted to just pack everything up and move to LA. We probably would have too, except Stew was about halfway through with his MBA and didn't want to lose credits by transferring to a school out there.

So back then it was California and now it was Calgary. The only problem was that Canada is very protective of its job market; it's very difficult for someone from the United States to get a Canadian work visa. In the area of broadcasting, it's practically impossible.

I decided that if I couldn't work in Calgary, then Seattle would be the next best thing. Back when I had been in Calgary, I became friendly with Shelly, a freelance producer for ABC, and the whole time we were there I was telling her how much I loved Calgary and how I wished I could get a job there. Shelly lived in Seattle, and she said Seattle was a lot like Calgary. She suggested I go out to visit her after the Olympics and arrange to meet with the news directors at the five TV stations out there and hand-deliver my audition tape to them.

This was easier said than done because, well, I didn't have an audition tape. Although I'd been working in TV for several years now, I hadn't done any TV sports since I had left Channel

55, well over a year before. Most recently I'd been doing fill-in news anchoring at News 12, but, like New York Tech, they felt it was too much of a risk to have a woman do sports on TV.

Although I had some old tapes from Channel 55, I couldn't use them for three main reasons: (1) The sports stories were outdated, (2) I was much better in front of the camera now than I had been back then, and (3) the lighting on the Channel 55 set was, well, let's just say it made me look like I had a face best suited for radio.

I wasn't going to let a little thing like not having a decent audition tape stop me from getting to Seattle. This was my dream! Well, at least it was my dream of the moment, and I was going to do whatever it took to make it come true.

What it took was fifty dollars and two baskets of fresh-baked chocolate chip cookies given to the crew at News 12 Long Island to convince them to help me make my tape. After the crew agreed to help me, I reviewed the most recent sports video, put together an extended sportscast for my tape, and headed out to Seattle. When I arrived, Shelly loaned me her car and I made the rounds of all the local TV stations.

Then I waited. Then I waited some more. And then I waited some more. Then I decided that it was probably going to take more than an audition tape and a smile to get a full-time job in TV. I needed an agent.

I was fairly well known in the industry now, especially in New York, where there were lots of agents, and I figured, how hard could it be to find someone who was willing to take 10 percent of my salary?

The answer was that it was very hard. I was actually having a harder time finding an agent than I ever had finding a job. I was making phone calls and following up on leads from people I knew, but no one wanted to take a chance and represent me. I thought I was doing quite well, but most agents, it seems, didn't think I was worth their time.

Frustrated with the seemingly impossible task of finding an agent and with what I saw as the stalling of my career, the confusion I had buried after coming back from Calgary surfaced again. Stew was still the same person I had met in college, but our lives seemed so boring compared with back then. I just didn't think I wanted to be married anymore, to anyone. I wanted to be a fun and free-spirited single woman who could do whatever she wanted without worrying about anyone else. At least that's how I felt most of the time. Other times I thought I was crazy to even think of leaving Stew. He had been the best thing that ever happened to me.

I kept going back and forth on this married/not married thing for a while, but whenever I looked at it hard, it didn't seem like being married was the right thing. Finally, on a night when Stew and I were both home, I confronted him and said I didn't think I wanted to be married anymore. For good measure, I added the old reliable "It's not you, it's me" line.

Stew was furious. He just didn't understand how I could, all of a sudden, not want to be married anymore. The way he saw it, we had been going out for six years before we got married and then, after being married for less than three years, I wanted out. What had changed over the last two and a half years that I couldn't have figured out in the six years before that?

I wasn't sure what had changed, all I knew was how I felt. The way *I* saw it, I had to be honest with him. I couldn't make believe everything was all right when it wasn't. I wasn't going to lie to him, and I wasn't going to fake it.

After he blew off some steam, he told me he thought we should see a marriage counselor. I told him that I already had one picked out—a friend of mine had recommended someone to me—and that if he wanted to see him too, that would be okay with me. Part of me wanted to be done with the whole thing, but another part of me felt I owed it to Stew, and myself, to at least try to work things out.

For the next two or three days, I don't think Stew said more than a couple of words to me. He felt I hadn't ever taken our marriage seriously and wasn't making an effort. I felt that if we were meant to be together, I shouldn't have to work at it. That made him even angrier.

What finally opened up the lines of communication again was that, at the end of the week, my younger sister, Donna, was coming to spend the summer with us, so Stew had to figure out a way to get over his anger. He was too considerate a guy to put Donna in the middle of our marital problems.

While my home life was in shambles, my career was starting to look up again. After months of looking, I connected with an independent female agent who said she wanted to meet with me. I thought this would be great. Who would be able to understand my situation better than another woman?

The meeting started off well enough at a fancy restaurant she had picked out not too far from the ABC studios where I worked. I was impressed that such an upscale agent was interested in representing me, but once we got down to business I could see that my impression had been all wrong. This so-called agent wanted me to do all the legwork, track down the leads, make the initial contacts with the stations, and sell myself to them. If I could do that, then what did I need an agent for?

But maybe I was wrong. I had never had an agent before. Perhaps that's how it worked. By the end of the meal, though, when she stuck me with the check at the high-priced restaurant she had picked out, I knew the only thing wrong was her. Oh well, back to the drawing board.

Without an agent, my strategy was to send out tapes to as many stations in the top ten US markets as possible. Because I worked for ABC, it was easy to follow up at any station with a phone call. All I had to do was tell the receptionist that I was from ABC, and they would connect me with a higher-up at the station. This was a critical benefit for me. If I was ever going to get a job in TV, I'd have to stay in regular contact with these people so that, when they needed to fill a sports position, my name would come up for consideration automatically.

Back at home, Stew and I started seeing the therapist. The first thing I learned in therapy was, when picking a therapist, never take the recommendation of someone who doesn't seem to be better-adjusted than you are. I don't want to reveal anything specific about my friend's affliction, but let's just say therapy didn't seem to be helping him any.

After looking back on my own experience with this therapist—for convenience, I'll call him Larry the Therapist—I could see why my friend wasn't getting any better. Stew and I started off by seeing him individually, and a typical session between Larry and me would consist mainly of us talking about sports and him telling me what a great job I was doing. Larry was totally feeding into my celebrity and the thrill of being able to talk sports with a woman. Rather than helping me to thoughtfully address the issues I was facing, he was pumping up my ego and, in effect, telling me to stay just the way I was and not compromise on anything.

Larry's advice to Stew, in comparison, was that I was a woman who needed a lot of excitement and stimulation in my life and that he needed to be more exciting. This was turning out to be a pretty good situation for me. I got to talk about sports for fifty minutes while my husband was being given an instruction manual on how to cater to my need for constant excitement.

This went on for about a month until Stew's brother, Bob, who was also a therapist, suggested we might have a better chance of solving our relationship problems if we saw Larry together. Now, why didn't Larry think of that?

Stew made the suggestion to our therapist, and he reluctantly agreed to give it a try. We saw him together as a couple for six months. The one valuable insight we got from him, seriously, was that Stew was always shutting me down.

I had never realized it, because it was so out of character with the rest of Stew's personality, but whenever Stew and I disagreed about something, Stew would raise his voice and interrupt me in the middle of a sentence; I would just shut down and go along with whatever he said. It's hard to have an open and honest relationship when one person doesn't get the chance, for whatever reason, to be heard.

To his credit, Stew recognized his problem once it was pointed out to him and worked hard to change. For my part, I recognized that my shutting down was due, in part, to years of trying to avoid the wrath of my mother's tirades. I had to start standing up for myself.

I don't want to mitigate the value of that insight, because it did significantly improve our ability to communicate with each other and work through future issues, but that was basically the only thing we learned from Larry. Otherwise, it was pretty much Larry giving me lots of positive reinforcement and telling Stew that he needed to work harder to make me happy.

Still, over the next few months I was starting to feel that closeness and comfort with Stew I thought I had lost. Perhaps despite our so-called therapy, spending an hour each week together just talking about us and focusing on our relationship helped us regain that emotional intimacy. After each session, we'd go out for a nice dinner. Therapy was actually becoming fun. After six months, I was feeling good about everything again, and I told Stew we didn't need to see Larry anymore.

In my career everything remained status quo . . . and I hate status quo. I was continuing to send out audition tapes and make phone calls every few months to touch base with those stations I'd already sent out tapes to, but nothing was happening. It wasn't that I was losing jobs to other candidates; there just weren't any jobs out there to lose.

I also wasn't having any luck finding an agent who wanted to take me on. It seemed to me that I was in a slump, although, in reality, a lot of people would have given anything to be in my shoes: a full-time position at the ABC Entertainment Network with the opportunity to do fill-in work at WABC, WFAN, and News 12.

Finally I caught a bit of a break when I got a callback from Peter Goldberg, a young agent with one of the bigger sports agencies in town. He was familiar with my work and expressed interest in representing me.

Although his agency wouldn't let him offer me a contract, Peter was a big believer in my potential and felt he could get me a full-time TV position. He started working for me right away, but ran into the same roadblocks I did.

Then, one day, he called to say he had heard back from a station in North Carolina that was very interested in me. They had sent him a tape of a recent sportscast, and he was sending it over for me to look at it. He said, if I was interested, he was pretty sure he could get me the job.

When the tape came, Stew and I sat down together to watch it, and we were both pretty excited. I had gone from having no agent and no full-time TV prospects to having a legitimate, net-work affiliate station send *me* an audition tape.

After watching the tape, I was much less excited, to say the least, but I wanted to see what Stew thought.

I said, "So what do you think?"

Stew said, "I don't know. Did you notice that the number one sports story was a tractor pull contest?"

Not that there's anything wrong with tractor pulls. Living in central Connecticut, I've been exposed to my share of them at local fairs. It's just that I didn't think I wanted to work in an area where the best and most exciting sports story the station could come up with was which local farmer pulled a 10-ton sled 20 feet in the shortest amount of time. As much as I was enticed by a full-time position at a network affiliate, I knew I would be miserable there. I had to turn down the job.

I didn't get another job offer for six months.

Then in the late spring of 1989, I got a call from John Lippman, the news director at KIRO-TV in Seattle. KIRO—the CBS affiliate—was one of the stations I had visited almost a year earlier. Now, after countless *Anything new?* calls, there was an opening for a sports reporter.

Like everything else in my career, the job at KIRO came to me through a combination of perseverance, luck, and hard work. John Lippman was a progressive-thinking news director, and the idea of hiring a woman to cover sports was one he actively pursued. I didn't have to convince him that a woman was capable of delivering a credible sportscast on TV. I just had to convince him that I was that woman.

Within a few weeks of receiving that first phone call from John, I had flown out to Seattle for a live audition, been offered the job, gone back out there with Stew to find an apartment, and given my notice to WABC.

While the only thing that had come to Stew's mind about Seattle before I was offered the job at KIRO was the old *Here Come the Brides* television show, he was as ready to leave New York as I was. Although we lived only 7 miles from his office, between the walk to the subway and the ride on two different subway trains, it took him almost an hour to get to work each day.

We also lived in a pre–Rudolph Giuliani New York, and were both tired of the general hardness of the city and the commonplace crime. Our apartment had been burglarized once and our car had been broken into as well. Car break-ins were so common in our neighborhood; we didn't even bother reporting ours to the police. Instead, like our neighbors, we dealt with petty car break-ins by keeping our glove compartment open and our car doors unlocked so that passing criminals could easily check to make sure there was nothing in the car worth stealing. Maybe there was something wrong with making the lives of criminals easier, but it was better than continually having to replace mangled car locks and broken side windows.

In early October, without any regrets, we boarded a Piedmont Airlines jet and flew out to Seattle. Ten hours later—including a three-hour delay in Atlanta—we passed through two separate layers of clouds into a dark and drizzly Seattle. Except for being a little warmer, it reminded us a lot of Oswego. In a way it was like coming home. We couldn't wait.

FIVE

Go West Young Lady

In Seattle, there is a closely knit secret organization called the Lesser Seattle Society. It is so secretive and dedicated to its sacred mission that I fear I may be risking my life simply by mentioning it here. The society has spies everywhere, and I'm afraid I might come to some permanent harm before I am able to send this chapter off to my publisher. Certainly, by the time you read this, the society will have begun seeking its retribution upon me and I will need to go into hiding. When you don't see or hear me on the air for a while, you'll know why.

Well, no. There really isn't any secret society, and my life isn't in any more danger than it usually is from the errant viewer who wants to kill me because I've personally offended him by saying something he didn't like about his beloved team. Just the same, there really is a quasi-serious, Lesser Seattle movement started long ago by Emmett Watson, a Seattle-based journalist.

Outwardly, the mission of the movement is to emphasize the negative aspects of Seattle—the rain and clouds, the ten-month heating season, the low pay, and the rain and clouds—to discourage outsiders from moving in and crowding up the place. Under the surface, though, it's a thinly veiled celebration of how wonderful a place Seattle is to live, and an acknowledgment by Seattleites of how lucky they are to live there.

Sure, Seattle isn't for everyone, but if you can get past the 300 cloudy days and the 150 days of rain they have each year, it can be a wonderful place to live. Seriously. The summers are sunny and dry, the city is friendly and fun, and there is an over-all celebration of the simpler things in life. I think you know what I mean by the "simpler things in life." Those are all the things that I usually think of as "boring."

Ever since I crawled out from behind my glasses, or even before then, I haven't been much of a fan of the simpler things in life. I've always wanted to be doing something, achieving some goal. Taking a break to stop and smell the roses was something I considered a waste of time. Even when I was forced into a situation where slowing down seemed like the whole purpose, I managed to turn it into a competition. Here's an example.

The fall before Stew and I moved to Seattle, we took a mini-vacation to Manchester, Vermont. In between stuffing our faces with pancakes and Vermont maple syrup, and talking a local restaurant owner into keeping his bar open all afternoon so we could watch the Mets battle the Dodgers in the NLCS, we decided to actually step outside and take a 3-mile hike up the side of a lush, tree-covered mountain.

The innkeeper at the lodge we were staying in told us we should allow two to three hours to climb the steep incline and enjoy the majestic view once we reached the top of the moun-tain. "You're going to want to give yourself enough time to really appreciate it," he said.

I thought, *Yeah, whatever.* We drove to the mountain, parked, and as soon as we got to the trailhead, I was making tracks, pulling Stew—who's much more of a nature lover than I am—along behind me as fast as he would go. We made the two- to three-hour climb up the mountain in just about an hour. It was a beautiful fall day, so there were a lot of nature-loving slowpokes in our way, and more than a few of them gave us disdainful, sideways glances as we forced past them on the narrow trail. But I didn't care. I knew they thought I was crazy, but I thought they were crazy too. I came to the mountain, I saw the mountain, I conquered the mountain. Wasn't that the point? That's what I thought.

When we got to the top of the mountain, I took in the scenery, looked at Stew, and said, "Wow, this is cool. I'm done. Let's go." Then we climbed back down the mountain looking for something else to do. Having achieved the goal, I was bored and ready to move on.

So it was as much of a surprise to me as to anyone else when we moved to Seattle and I found myself actually enjoying the simple pleasures in life. It made it a really good time for Stew and me. No, I'm not saying Stew was a simple pleasure. I'm saying that when you appreciate the simple things in life together, you also appreciate each other.

Are you with me yet? What I'm trying to say is, we both loved Seattle and we relished just spending time together there. One of our favorite things to do was go down to Gas Works Park with a couple of take-out dinners from the nearby teriyaki place and watch the boats sail around Lake Union. If that's not enjoying the little things in life, I don't know what is. For me to sit in one spot watching anything that didn't involve a scoreboard was unheard of.

A few months later we bought our first house. A little two-bedroom on the top of Queen Anne Hill with a white picket fence and a couple of cherry trees in the backyard.

In the spring I filled the window boxes and planters in front with all types of flowering plants—geraniums, petunias, begonias, hanging ivies, pansies, and Johnny-jump-ups—and watered them every day. It's the only time in my life that the plants I was taking care of didn't die from neglect.

After we bought the house, another thing we liked to do was wake up Sunday mornings, walk two blocks to the neighborhood bakery, and sit at a table on the sidewalk sipping lattes and eating scones. This was way before Starbucks had spread the joy of espresso drinks beyond the borders of Seattle, and I was enamored with the jolt of a caffeine-laced latte. I don't know what I liked more, the lattes, the scones, or just sitting outside sharing the morning together.

It was at one of those little caffeine fuel-ups that Stew said, "I love Seattle so much. I don't ever want to leave."

And I said, "Yeah. Me too. It's great here. The only way I would ever leave is if I were offered a job at ESPN. That would be my dream job."* But the possibility of that actually happening seemed so unlikely, we just smiled at each other and took another sip from our lattes.

All right, I'm done with that touchy-feely stuff for now. Let's get to how things were going at my first job as a sports reporter for a network affiliate station. Well, I'm happy to say, things were going pretty well, despite the fact that I had been hired, as I later found out, against the sports director's better judgment.

Apparently, what happened was that John Lippman, the news director at KIRO, went into the sports director's office,

---

* If you're wondering, "Isn't *Dream Job* the name of a reality show on ESPN?" you're right, but that's exactly what I said.

dumped a pile of audition tapes on his desk, and said, "Here are a bunch of audition tapes we've received. Pick out two that you like and we'll interview them for the new sports reporter job."

The sports director, Steve Raible, dutifully spent the better part of a day going through all the tapes and picked out two guys he thought looked good on the air and seemed to know their stuff. Neither of those "guys" was me.

Here's how Steve remembers it: "I walked into John's office with the two tapes and told him why I thought we should bring these two guys out to interview. John took it all in, looked straight at me, and said 'That's nice. I think I'm going to hire Linda Cohn.' And I thought, *Great, I just spent almost a whole day going through all these tapes and now John tells me that of all the people looking to get a job at KIRO, we're going to hire a girl from Long Island with almost no TV experience.*"

It would probably make a more interesting story if I could tell you about how Steve was resentful of John's executive decision and took it out on me, but that wasn't the case: "Whatever I felt about the way John handled things, the guy had an eye for talent and I had to accept that. What I wanted was someone who could be part of a team, and you knew how to do that. But part of being a team was also knowing how to go out on your own and learn things on your own. And you could do that too."

Steve didn't only talk a good story, he had lived through one of his own. He was one of the original wide receivers for the Seattle Seahawks; when an off-field injury caused him to retire in 1981, he beat the odds by talking KIRO-TV into taking a chance and hiring him as a sportscaster and alternate to Seattle legend Wayne Cody. Back then, and even more so nowadays, while many former athletes can parlay their way into an on-air analyst position, they are almost never hired as anchors. Not only did Steve make the transition to sports anchor, but, by the time I got there, he was, as you already know, sports director. By the way, Steve now coanchors the news for KIRO's prime-time *Eyewitness News* and is a play-by-play announcer for the Seahawks at KIRO radio.

While Steve was ready to accept me with open arms, Wayne Cody was not. Wayne was an icon in Seattle and widely known, affectionately, as the Mound of Sound, as much for his size as for the rich timbre of his voice. He was also known for his fun-loving on-air personality. He once did a sportscast in a pumpkin suit; another time, in a hot tub. I wasn't in Seattle then, but picture a man hovering around 300 pounds, *without* a football player's physique, in a hot tub. It had to be funny, I guess. Well, anyway, Wayne might have liked to have fun, but he sure didn't seem to like me.

By this time I had figured out that if I was going to be in broadcasting, I was going to have to develop a thick skin. I think it's a general rule that if you're going to make an impact in TV, or in whatever you do, you're probably going to end up with some people who don't like you. I knew not everyone who saw me on TV was going to be a fan, and I was fine with that. But I wasn't fine with being disliked by one of the only two other people doing sports at the station, especially if that person was the Mound of Sound. To not get, at the very least, his polite tolerance made it uncomfortable for me, even though I knew I wasn't the only one at the station he had a problem with.

I know I'm going to get myself in trouble with some people here, but I'm pretty sure another reason Wayne kept a wall between the two of us was because he was afraid that if we ever got into a friendly conversation over sports, it would be obvious to everyone that the new woman they had hired from New York knew more than the famous Wayne Cody. By his own admission, Wayne always considered himself more of an entertainer than a sportscaster—hence the pumpkin suit and the hot tub—and he had been quoted as saying that he knew a little about a lot of things. Still, he was definitely a good ol' boy, and I think the prospect of being shown that he knew less about sports than a woman—even a woman who had dedicated the last eleven years of her life to sportscasting—was more than he was willing to accept.

Not that I was interested in showing him up or even comparing myself to him in any way. I was too concerned with just trying to demonstrate to Steve and John that it hadn't been a mistake to hire me.

My first assignment at KIRO was to do a "live shot" at the Key Arena before a Sonics game. It was the first time I had ever done a live shot, although Steve probably didn't realize this, and I was seriously afraid that I was going to screw it up.

A live shot is, simply, a live report from a remote location. It's just you, the cameraman, and a barrage of voices from the studio in your ear. I knew *how* to do a live shot, but I also knew there was a big difference between knowing how to do a live shot and actually doing it on the air. Instead of following my own advice and trying just to do my best, I kept thinking about everything that could go wrong. It was all stupid stuff—*What if I miss the cue from the anchor in my earpiece and just stand in front of the camera like a deer in headlights? What if I forget to throw back to the studio when I'm done with my report? What if I forget what I'm supposed to say or start stumbling over my words? Why does my very first live shot ever have to be in front of the largest six o'clock news audience in Seattle? Oh my God!* I was freaking out and I knew it. If I didn't settle down, I was definitely going to screw up.

So I called the voice of experience, my friend Lea Tyrell, the news anchor at News 12 Long Island, in a panic. As soon as she picked up the phone and said "Hello" I went off for what seemed like forever, explaining when and where I was doing the live shot, how I had prepared, why I had prepared the way I had, how I was feeling, why I was nervous, what I was nervous about, how I didn't think I was going to be able to get through this, and how I didn't know what I was going to do. When I finally stopped to take a deep breath, Lea very slowly and calmly said, "Don't worry. It's not a big deal. You know your stuff and you can do this. Just make believe you're with me and we're in the arena waiting for the Sonics game to start. When you do your stand-up, imagine we're just talking between the two of us and I asked you to tell me what to expect in the game."

It was exactly what I needed: a simple solution and the reassurance of a trusted friend. After getting off the phone with Lea, I was able to calm down and concentrate on what I was supposed to be doing. I stopped worrying about how many different ways there were for me to screw up; and when I got the cue in my ear to start my report, I visualized myself having a conversation with Lea, even though she was 3,000 miles away, and everything was fine. Everything, that is, except that the cameraman had accidentally used a modified fish-eye lens on his camera. Have you ever tried to look at yourself in the reflection of a polished door knob? That's what I looked like to Seattle viewers the first time they saw me on TV.

But I got over it. I got over it, mainly, because I was beginning to realize that I had to let go of things I couldn't change, but also because everything else—well, nearly everything else—was going so well. Although Steve Levy, who had been a colleague of mine at the FAN and is now a colleague of mine at ESPN, questioned me as to why I would want to leave the number one broadcast market in the world to go all the way to Seattle (the fourteenth market), it had been the right move for me.

For one thing, since there were only two newspapers and three local news teams in the area, there was a kind of brotherhood—or once I got there, I guess it became a sister/brotherhood—among the same four or five sports reporters I saw at whatever game I was covering. With my New York accent, I stood out like a sore thumb, especially during interviews, since that's when the whole "speak slowly" thing I had learned from Fritz went out the window, and my accent really came out. But it didn't matter. All the reporters were very easygoing, and they weren't judging me or my accent. I think they figured if I was smart enough to want to live in Seattle, then I had to be okay. They just all seemed to have an attitude of acceptance and a lack of ego.

That attitude wasn't found just among people in my industry, but seemed to permeate all walks of life. It wasn't unusual, for instance, to be at one of the city's many festivals and see a clean-cut businessman in a suit and a forty-year-old hippie in long hair and thrift store clothes standing side by side, grooving to the same band and talking to each other. Refreshingly, there just wasn't much of an emphasis placed on class distinctions. Most people were more interested in living a good life than acquiring status symbols or comparing themselves with one another.

Remarkably, that lack of ego also extended to the professional athletes who played in Seattle. Although Seattle was a
city of half a million people, it acted, in many ways, like a small
town. Similar to my experience with the Islanders, there was a
familiarity between the athletes and the fans, only more so. In
Seattle athletes weren't considered celebrities so much as they
were considered the guys in the town who represented us in
baseball and basketball and football.

Shortly after moving to Seattle, I was in Tower Records
when I noticed Randy Johnson, who was pitching for the Mari-
ners at the time, looking over CDs. Since he's 6 foot 10, it was
hard for me *not* to notice him. I walked over, introduced myself,
and asked him, matter-of-factly, what he was doing. He told me
he was looking for some of the later Beatles albums to round
out his CD collection. I told him what a big Beatles nut I was,
and we talked about the White Album for a while. Then we
went our separate ways. As we said our good-byes, I told him
I looked forward to covering him in the spring. That was the
only time during the conversation either one of us even referred
to baseball. Otherwise, we were just two people with a mutual
interest in music.

While I had no problem finding something in common with
Randy Johnson, my interactions with Wayne Cody back at KIRO
were becoming close to intolerable. At work I was keeping on
my Miss Happy face, but one night I loaded all my frustration
on Stew. After all, he was my husband. Wasn't that his job?

"I've been trying to deal with this on my own, but I don't
know what else to do. Wayne just doesn't seem to like me."

Stew wasn't just my husband. I knew that, among his own
colleagues, he had a reputation for being able to get along with

just about anyone. What I wasn't ready to hear from him, though, was that getting along with difficult people usually meant compromising on things you didn't think you should compromise on. I didn't like it.

"Wayne probably sees you as a threat. I think you just have to reach out to him. Go out of your way to be nice to him, show him who you really are and that you're not a threat. Once he gets to know who you really are, everything should be fine."

"But I never did anything to make him think that I was a threat. It's not my fault! Why do I have to make the effort? It's not fair! He's the one who's got things all wrong. He's the one who should be reaching out to me."

"Look, lots of times a woman who is strong and confident at work is seen as a bitch. If you were a man, it would be different, but you're a woman. It's not fair, but that's the way it is. You can either live with things the way they are or you can try and make them better. It's your choice."

"Okay, so I'll just be a phony. I'll make believe I think he's the greatest thing to walk this earth. I'll tell him how great he is."

"I didn't say be a phony. I said reach out to him. Like I said, give him a chance to get to know you. Open the door. Let down your defenses so he can see who you really are."

I so did not want to be the one to give in on this, but I didn't see that I had any other choice. I followed Stew's advice. If Wayne was abrupt with me, instead of being offended, I would try to engage him in a conversation. If I was working in the newsroom and Wayne came in without acknowledging me, instead of following his lead and playing a game of silent treatment with him, I would look up and give him a friendly smile and a hello. Instead of treating him the way I thought he should be treated based on his behavior, I treated him the way I wanted him to treat me. And it worked.

Within a week or two, our relationship changed from one of reluctant coworkers to one of appreciative colleagues. No, Wayne never invited me over to his house to watch the Super Bowl, but we did develop a friendly rapport at work that usually, surprise, revolved around sports.

Ever since that experience, I've taken the lesson I learned with Wayne to heart and used it over and over again to change negative relationships into positive ones. Throughout my career I've been very lucky to encounter people, who, for the most part, have accepted me at face value. But every now and then, I've run into good people who expect the worst from me.

Some of it comes with the territory of being a woman in a male-dominated field. In at least one case that I know of, it arose from being bad-mouthed by someone who wanted my job. Whatever the reason, it doesn't really matter.

What does matter is that I've come to realize I'm never going to change someone's mind about me by reflecting their negativity. If I do, I'm just showing them what they expect. The only way I've found to prove people wrong is to let my defenses down and reach out to them. I've realized people can't see the real me unless I let them.

Of course, there are some people who aren't going to like what they see no matter what you show them, and that's something I learned a few months later when John Lippman gave me the weekend sports anchor position. I was replacing John Procaccino, who was also an accomplished actor and was hugely popular among both viewers and coworkers. You know the type: funny, engaging, the life of the party wherever he goes.

John was being moved from the sports anchor position to entertainment anchor. When the news came down from the top that I would be replacing him, he came up to me, wished me luck, and said he thought I would do a great job. I could tell from the look in his eyes that he meant it. I think he would have liked to have continued being the weekend sports anchor, but he wasn't going to blame me for what happened. Knowing that John was actually rooting for me took a load off my mind, and I'm sure he knew that too.

With the sign from John that everything was okay between us, I was ready for my first sports anchoring shift at KIRO. I was a little nervous, but definitely not anywhere near as nervous as when I had done my first live shot, and my first shift went off without a hitch.

A few days later I woke up before work and walked over to the Starbucks down the street to get a latte and read the sports section of the paper. Except for those few years when I was doing news, I almost never looked at anything but the back of the newspaper. The front of the paper is always too depressing for me; sports are about as much of the real world as I can handle most days.

So there I was, reading the sports section, like I did almost every morning, when I noticed the paper had added a Letters to the Editor feature to the sports section. *What a great idea,* I thought. I liked to hear what other fans were thinking about, so I read it to find out what was going on in the minds of other Seattleites. What I found out was, apparently, that other sports fans thought Linda Cohn was the worst sports anchor they had ever seen in Seattle and that KIRO should bring back John Procaccino. There were only two or three letters, and all of them were bashing me. Good thing I had already come to the realization that not everyone was going to like me.

What was most interesting to me, as I mentioned, was that I had never seen a letter to the editor in the sports section before that day and, for as long as I lived in Seattle, I never saw one again. Curiously, the letters, as I recall, were anonymous, even though newspapers don't usually print anonymous letters to the editor. I'm not one to be paranoid, but when something like this happens, you have to wonder.

Other than that, my transition to weekend sports anchor went through without a hitch. Despite the anonymous letters, Jim Moore, a columnist for the same paper, gave me a favorable review. I was starting to feel very comfortable at KIRO and was having a great time doing my job.

That doesn't mean I didn't have some on-the-job training to do. I certainly made my share of mistakes. For instance, there was the time I filled almost my entire sportscast with hockey highlights—a sport that, as we all know, I love, but that almost no one in Seattle cared about. After the show John Lippman called Steve and essentially banned me from ever showing another hockey highlight as long as I worked for him.

Then there was the night I was reviewing the highlight tapes for my show on the library video machine. Although I didn't always have time, I liked to review the tapes whenever I could because, if I knew exactly what was coming up in the show, I could add a bit more information and maybe tell my viewers something they had never heard before.

My mistake on this night was using the machine in the library, because it was in the library for a reason: It didn't work. Oh, it played tapes all right, but unbeknownst to me, when I rewound each tape and cued it up for the show, it automatically rewound another full minute before ejecting. So when I started my show, I had eight miscued tapes, but didn't know it.

During my sportscast, whenever I threw to a highlight, it started in the wrong place. The first highlight I threw to was a Pistons–Knicks game. Not only was it the wrong highlight, it was the wrong game. The tape had rewound all the way back to a previous game that was still on there, and the Pistons were wearing their away uniforms instead of their home attire.

When I saw what was happening, my first thought was that someone had put in the wrong tape. I had no idea that *all* the tapes were miscued. I took a deep breath and said to the camera, "Okay. That's obviously not tonight's game. Let's go to the next highlight." But the next highlight wasn't any better, and neither was the one after that. I kept thinking, *If I can just get to the next highlight, I'll be okay.* But every new highlight was as wrong as the one before it. I began to wonder if someone was trying to sabotage my show.

When I finally got off the set, after eight wrong highlights, I didn't know whether I wanted to find and kill the person responsible or just sit down and cry. Dave Reese, my producer, saw the fire in my eyes and pulled me aside before I had a chance to embarrass myself. As he was watching the show, he had realized what the problem was. He gently explained to me why the machine I had used was in the library, and why nobody ever used it.

Every anchor gets hung out to dry now and then; it's just something you have to learn to get through as best you can. Usually it's due to everyone rushing around trying to get a live show done on time the best way they can, and you learn to accept that. But when you find out that you're the one who left yourself out to dry, that's hard to swallow. Lucky for me, I had Dave and he knew the cure. Good company and a Rainier Beer at Duke's before I headed home.

Three months later, and with no other major mishaps to speak of, I received a call from Peter. You remember Peter. He was the one agent who expressed any faith that I could make it as a TV sportscaster (even though his agency didn't seem to share this feeling). I had gotten the job at KIRO on my own—along with a little help from Shelly—so I didn't owe Peter anything, legally or ethically.

Just the same, when I got the job, I decided to pay Peter his standard 10 percent commission as a sign of good faith. After all, he'd had faith in me. It ended up paying off, because his call six months later was to tell me that ESPN was interested in talking to me!

Within a week I hopped a plane to Connecticut and was interviewing with the bigwigs in Bristol. After the interview I felt like I had really impressed them, and I must have been right, because a week later Peter called to tell me they wanted to fly me back out for another set of interviews; there was a good chance they would make me a job offer before I left.

When I told Stew the good news, he said, "I didn't quit my job and move 3,000 miles to Seattle just so I could move back six months later."

I was stunned! This was my dream job. It was the culmination of everything I had been working toward for almost nine years. But Stew was adamant, and there was no changing his mind. Actually, he did have a point. Although he had been more than ready to go out west, he had left a fast-track job in New York and moved to Seattle with almost no job prospects at all, just so I could get my first full-time job in TV. Then, once he finally did get a job after months of frustration, I told him I wanted him to quit again, leave a city that we'd both fallen in love with, and move back east.

So I ended up calling Peter and having him tell ESPN that my husband had just started a new job and we couldn't move. Usually I would have dwelled forever on a missed opportunity like that, but I think I loved Seattle so much I just let it go. Peter said that when he told ESPN why I wasn't coming back for a second interview, they liked that I was putting my family before my career. They told him they would leave the door open for me to come back and interview again in the future.

Being a sports anchor, even a weekend sports anchor, in a small city like Seattle, I started feeling like a celebrity pretty quickly. All the athletes from the local teams knew who I was, and I never had any trouble getting an interview with any of them. Around town, I was often recognized and, I have to say, I was beginning to bask in my own semi-stardom.

I've never been the type to think of myself as better than anyone else, but, as you've probably learned, I do like to be the center of attention. Now, just to put things in perspective, it wasn't like I couldn't walk down the street without getting mobbed. After all, I was just a weekend sports anchor in a city of people not all that impressed by celebrities. Even so, I was getting recognized now and then, and I loved the attention.

That spring I was asked to participate in my first charity event. Bob Gilmore, the owner of the research firm Stew was working for, asked if I would help him out with a charity he was involved with. He had been given tickets to the Goodwill Games and wanted to auction them off as part of a package that included me accompanying the winning bidders to the games and providing them with a seat-side commentary.

My entry in the list of auction items said something like this:

> **An Evening with Linda Cohn and the Goodwill Games**
> *Experience your own personal, play-by-play commentary when Linda Cohn, weekend sports anchor for KIRO-TV, accompanies you to the Goodwill Games.*

I know, it's not that impressive, but just to see the listing was a thrill for me. It probably sounds funny to you that someone who was on TV five days a week (three days reporting and two days anchoring) would get excited about being listed in an auction pamphlet that was being seen by only a few hundred people, but to me it meant I was a big enough star that someone thought they could use my celebrity status to help them raise money for their cause. It was a major external validation of my worth and, as shallow as it might seem, I was all about external validation.

One of the items auctioned off before me was dinner at a local four-star restaurant with one of the players from the Sonics basketball team. Embarrassingly, he only raised a few hundred dollars, and he was a big star. I started to get nervous. If a Sonics basketball player could only raise a few hundred dollars, what chance did someone who only talked about basketball have? What if my opportunity for external validation turned out validating that I wasn't worth very much after all?

When it was finally my turn up at the auction block, bidding started off slow at $25, but gradually picked up and finished at about $1,200.

I did the calculations in my head. The four tickets to the Goodwill Games were worth about $200 total, which meant they were able to raise an additional $1,000 just because of me.

That was respectable, I thought. I excused myself from the table and went over to meet the winning bidder so we could get to know each other before we went to the Goodwill Games together.

"Hi! Thanks for bidding on me," I said with a little laugh. "I thought it would be nice to talk a little bit before we went to the games together. You won me, so I'll be completely at your beck and call when we go."

The winning bidder looked at me and said, "Oh. I don't even know who you are. I just wanted to go to the Goodwill Games with my family and I thought, since I was donating to a good cause, why not spend the money. I don't care if you come with us or not."

That was painful, and most people would have learned their lesson from something like that, but not me. A few months later I was in the Pike Place Market when a guy walked up to me and said, "You look very familiar. Do I know you from somewhere?"

I put on my biggest smile, and said confidently, "You've probably seen me on TV. I'm Linda Cohn, the weekend sports anchor for KIRO."

"No, that's not it. I must be thinking of someone else," he said and walked away. That's when I finally learned my lesson about being too proud of myself. These days I'm much better at handling situations like that. If someone comes up to me, even if it looks like they know me, I always introduce myself by saying, "Hi. Linda Cohn." That way there's no doubt about who I am and there's no impression that I'm full of myself. (Really, I'm not. Well, not anymore.)

Now I'm going to tell you a story that I almost didn't include in the book because whenever I think about it, it leaves me confused, disturbed, and angry. Still, it was a traumatic experience in my life and, for this reason, I feel like it has to be included. It happened when I was living in Seattle and involved a player on one of Seattle's professional teams. Because of the events that occurred, I've done my best to mask the identity of the other person involved. However, as you'll see by the end of this story, I'm not sure if I'm protecting the innocent or the guilty. Either way, I'm not about to one-sidedly crucify someone who can't defend himself.

Okay, here it goes:

It was near the end of the season and I was doing interviews like I did after every game. Sometimes these interviews took place inside the locker room and sometimes outside, in a common meeting area. In this particular case we were doing our interviews in the common area. It was one of those situations where you tell the PR guy who you want to speak to, and that player comes over to do the interview when he's free. I had just finished an interview and was waiting for my next one to show up when "Mike"—another player—came walking by. Mike was a really nice guy, and he always seemed to make an extra effort to stop and say hi to me, even if we weren't doing an interview together.

As he walked by, I gave him a little wave and said, "Hi Mike," just like I always did. He turned his head toward me and came over to chat. I hadn't realized it yet, but he wasn't exactly in a chatting mood. He brushed past the other reporters, stood square in front of me, and started screaming at me at the top of his lungs. It was like one of those barrages of pure rage I remembered getting from my mother when I was a kid.

For a minute I couldn't understand what he was saying. He didn't even seem to be making sense. Or maybe I didn't understand him because it's hard to make sense out of anything when you have a hulking professional athlete towering over you with eyes filled with rage.

As I stood there frozen in front of him, I gradually pieced together enough of his words to realize he was angry at me for going into the locker room for an interview after the previous game. Was he kidding? That had been three days ago! Besides, I had been in the locker room so many times over the last few years without any incident that I didn't even think about it being an issue anymore.

Apparently, Mike did think about it, and he had been thinking about for at least three days, maybe longer. It wasn't just that he didn't think women belonged in the locker room. He thought that if a woman did go into the locker room, she was morally reprehensible, and he told me so in no uncertain terms, if you get my drift. At least I think he did. He was still barely comprehensible.

As you know, I'd been demeaned and berated about being in the locker room before—even though every major sport had ruled that it was a female reporter's right to have equal access—but this was different. To be told by someone like Mike, whom I had been interviewing and joking with for years, that the only reason I could possibly want to go into a men's locker room was because I wanted to offer myself up to one or more of his fellow players was shocking and unbelievable.

And to do something like that in front of the other players and reporters, all of whom I would have to continue to work with after this nightmare ended, was inexcusable. I looked around, but the other reporters were looking down at the ground. Either they were too embarrassed for me to look up, or they were thinking that I must have done something really bad for Mike to treat me this way.

What else were they supposed to think? No one would have guessed that amicable, even-tempered Mike would go off on me for something as inconsequential as doing an interview in the locker room.

I tried to explain to Mike that I was just doing my job, that I needed to go into the locker room so I could get the interviews I needed, but Mike yelled right through my explanation.

Then, as quickly as he had come over to begin his tirade, he left. Mike didn't seem interested in having a conversation with me and working things out; he just wanted to damn me to hell and leave. When he left, the room was completely still. There was a long, awkward silence. I was holding back my tears, but I knew they were going to come out in a floodstorm any second. Then I would be doubly embarrassed.

Just when I thought I wasn't going to be able to hold it together any longer, a few of Mike's teammates came over to tell me not to worry about Mike. He just had a problem, they said, and I should forget about it. To have the support of the other players made me feel a whole lot better. It also made it clear to my fellow reporters that I hadn't done anything wrong.

Later on, the PR guy came up to me and apologized also. "It's what he believes," the PR guy told me. Oh, is that supposed to make it all right? I see. It's okay for Mike to spew slanderous, sexist remarks at me in front of my colleagues and the team if it's "what he believes." I thought trying to justify that type of behavior with an excuse like that was almost worse than the behavior itself.

About a month later Mike was traded, although his being traded had nothing to do with what had happened that day. Even though he had made a public spectacle, I felt it was something between Mike and me, and I never brought it up to team management. I'm pretty sure he never did either.

For a while that seemed to be the end of the story. Then a few years later, I got a message from Mike through a mutual acquaintance. Mike was playing golf with this mutual acquaintance, whom we'll call Lou, when he brought up what had happened. Lou told me that Mike was genuinely sorry and that he had asked him to send his apologies to me.

I didn't know what to think. On the one hand, I was touched by the apology. I've done my own share of offending people, and when I apologize to someone, I really want them to know that I'm sorry, even if they don't forgive me. On the other hand, when I apologize to someone, I usually do it in person, or at least on the phone, not by asking someone I happened to be playing golf with to do it for me.

Over the years I had told a handful of people in the industry the story of Mike. I didn't do it to spread bad publicity about

Mike. That would serve no purpose. It was more of a catharsis for me but, regardless of my reasons, there were people in the industry who knew the story. I started thinking that maybe Mike wasn't really sorry. Maybe he had heard the story from someone else and wanted to nip it in the bud. I don't know what he was thinking, but in the end I decided I just had to forgive and forget the whole thing.

Except Mike didn't let me. A few years after that first apology, I received a note from Mike in the mail. This time he apologized in writing and asked if I would call him so we could clear the air once and for all. I was moved that Mike was still bothered enough after all this time to want to make things right, and I admired what I thought was a high level of ethics, but it was still painful and embarrassing for me to think about it. So I waited a few days to call him.

Then I noticed in the paper that Mike was running for a very public, national office. It made me wonder if he really was apologetic or merely trying to minimize the potential of any negative press. Not that I would ever say anything publicly that would affect his chances of election. What Mike had done was horrible, but I wasn't about to make a problem for him over a single incident that had happened so many years before.

Now I wasn't so sure if I wanted to call him or not. Eventually, he called me. I listened to his apology and accepted it for what it was, even though I wasn't sure what it was. With everything that had gone on, I couldn't decide if Mike was a man of deep character who couldn't rest until he put closure on a mistake from the past, or if he was a slimy soon-to-be politician who was only interested in keeping me quiet. I would never know because, a year later, he died tragically in an accident.

With no way of ever knowing whether or not Mike was genuinely sorry, I was left to come to terms with this whole thing on my own. What I finally did was put myself in Mike's position and forgive him. After all, the guy had apologized to me, twice. What more could he do? If that wasn't enough for me to accept that he was truly sorry, then maybe that said more about me than it did about him. And now, I think, I have gone through my final catharsis on this issue and I can finally put it to rest.

Like most couples, before Stew and I got married, we talked about whether or not we wanted children. At first Stew wanted two and I wanted three, but by the time we had moved to Seattle, I was down to "I'm not sure I want any kids at all." Stew still wanted two.

There were a lot reasons I didn't think I wanted kids—commitment, a signal that I wasn't young anymore, the feeling that I might be turning into my mother—but the biggest was that I was afraid I wouldn't be a good mother. I didn't feel like I had any motherly instinct. The truth was, I didn't even like kids all that much and I was afraid I was too selfish to give a child all the love he or she needed and deserved.

Seattle changed all that. I gained a broader perspective on life, got my head on straight, and realized I did want to have children. The question now was, when? Every time I looked at the calendar, the timing seemed wrong. Whenever I counted out nine months into the future, there was something going on that made it a less-than-ideal time to have a baby. I put the idea on hold.

A few months later I was on the road following the University of Washington Huskies to the NCAA women's basketball finals. On the way home from the tournament, I was talking with my cameraman, Matt, about how I'd finally decided that I wanted children but couldn't figure out when to do it.

Matt said, "I have two kids and I can tell you that there's never going to be an ideal time to have children. The right time to have children is when you have them. When they come, you'll make whatever changes in your life need to be made."

As usual, simple words that made sense. As I'm writing this book, I'm becoming a little embarrassed to realize that all of the major lessons I've learned in my life have been pretty simple ones. But isn't that how life is? Once you see the answer to something, it all seems pretty simple.

Anyway, then Matt said, "Besides, just because you want to get pregnant doesn't mean it's going to happen right away. Sometimes it takes awhile. It's not like you can say 'I want to give birth on March 12 so let's count back nine months and conceive on June 12.' You might not get pregnant for a few months, or longer."

I was good with the whole "never an ideal time" thing, but I wasn't so sure how I felt about "sometimes it takes a while." As you know, I wasn't used to letting nature take its course. I was more in the mind of, *I've decided to do something, now let's get this thing done.* It was the whole hike-up-the-mountain thing all over again.

Maybe you think that trying to have a baby should be a fun and joyful thing, but when I got home I was all business. I had a goal and I was going to do everything I could to reach it as soon as possible. I sat down with Stew and told him I was going to start taking my temperature to figure out when our best chance of getting pregnant was.

Stew looked at me like I was crazy. "Whoa, we haven't even tried yet. Why don't we just relax and see what happens. You know, sometimes just being uptight about it can lower your chances of getting pregnant."

He was right, of course. Just the same, I wanted to do what I could to stack the odds in my favor, so I did what every woman who wants to get pregnant right away does. I went to my brother.

Now, let me interrupt this story for a minute to give you a little background on my brother. Growing up in a household where my mother could erupt at any moment, and where anything Hank did to calm my mother down only made her more explosive, my brother was the anchor that held us all together. With a mix of sarcastic humor and common sense, Howie was able to add a sense of levity and laughter to any family crisis that would help us get through to the next day. He was also the only one in our house who could calm my mother down and get her to think semi-rationally. For that, and other reasons, to say that my sisters and I worshipped Howie is only a slight exaggeration.

Howie was also a chiropractor. So when he told me that he could adjust me to make me more fertile, I was all for it. Within a month I was pregnant. Stew and I were thrilled, and Stew, who is normally pretty humble, was playfully boastful about getting me pregnant so quickly. That is, until I pointed out to him that it was really my brother who was responsible.

"What!?" he asked.

"When Howie was up visiting, he examined me and said there was a problem with my ovaries. Then he gave me an adjustment so it would be easier for me to get pregnant."

"So I had nothing to do with it?"

"Of course you had something to do with it, honey, but Howie was the reason it happened so quickly."

We argued back and forth for a while and I finally decided to let it drop because I saw there was no way Stew and I were going to agree. Stew was always at odds with me about chiropractors and challenged everything Howie ever said anyway.

Back at KIRO, they told me I would be doing a new high school football highlights show on Friday nights called *Prep Locker Room*. High school football? I thought I was being punished. Coming from New York, with three local baseball teams, two local football teams, two local hockey teams, and two local basketball teams, there was very little interest in college sports, let alone high school.

But, as I've been saying, Seattle was different, and I was soon to find out that high school sports were *big time* in Seattle. They were so big that at the end of each high school season, the final championship game was played at the Kingdome. When *Prep Locker Room* debuted, it seemed like almost every high school football player, every parent, every cheerleader, and every high school football fan tuned in to watch. *Prep Locker Room* became the top-rated show for its time slot!

Dave and I had a ball putting it together too. Every Friday, after coming back from doing interviews at a couple of the games—and you could pretty much guarantee that, in Seattle, it would rain every Friday night during football season and frizz out my hair to the point that I looked like Roseanne Roseannadanna—I would come back to the studio, where Dave and I would track the various highlights to whatever popular music we wanted. After I learned how to pronounce the names of towns like Puyallup and Snoqualmie, it became one of my favorite shows to do.

The two things I liked most about it were the passion with which these boys played, and how excited they were when their game was highlighted on the show. One of the players I interviewed was Lawyer Milloy. You might recognize the name because he went on to become a four-time Pro Bowler and helped the Patriots win Super Bowl XXXVI. He came up to me at an ESPY Awards ceremony a few years back and said, "I don't know if you remember me. I'm Lawyer Milloy. Do you want to know something? I did my first-ever television interview with you when you were doing *Prep Locker Room,* and you made my mother so happy by putting it on! I just wanted to say thanks." If the show made that kind of impact on Lawyer Milloy and he remembered it all those years later, imagine what it meant to the other players. Maybe it sounds like a line from a bad song, but being able to give these players a thrill like that gave me a thrill as well.

High school football was not, however, without its controversies. Another player I interviewed for the show was a lineman named Ryan Padgett. In his senior year he ended up accepting a scholarship to play for Notre Dame, only it didn't work out the way he planned. Turns out, whoever was in charge of handing out scholarships at Notre Dame that year handed out too many, but didn't bother to tell Ryan that they were taking his back. So Ryan went out to Indiana for the big Notre Dame recruiting trip with his mom, and Lou Holtz came up to him and said, "Sorry son. We don't have a scholarship for you." And that was that.

Ryan was a formidable player, and he had been offered a number of scholarships from other good schools, but by the time he found out that his scholarship to Notre Dame was no good, the other schools had already offered those slots to other students. Ryan had to sit out the entire year.

By the time spring rolled around, many of the schools who had originally been interested in him weren't anymore. How could anyone know how he would play after missing an entire season? Eventually he managed to get into Northwestern University, a good school, but one known more for its academics than its football. Notre Dame and Northwestern weren't schools that played each other on a regular basis, but when they finally did, Ryan went out on the field with a personal mission to beat the team that had left him at the altar. It was a great victory for him, and we featured the story on *Prep Locker Room*. It was one of the best pieces to go on the résumé tape my agent sent over to ESPN a few months later.

When football season ended, my baby was just a little bump in my belly, but by baseball's spring training I was full-out preggo. In addition to the upcoming birth of my first child, it was nearing the fifteenth anniversary of the Kingdome. John Lippman, who was always thinking up new ways to keep the ratings high, had hatched a plan around the Kingdome anniversary that included me, seven months' pregnant, standing on its roof.

I loved that John was always thinking up new things for me to do. It made me feel like I was important to the show and that I was being used to my fullest potential. But this was a little crazy. I think John knew how crazy it was, because he didn't even tell me about it. He left that to Dave.

According to Dave, the way it happened was that he was walking down the hall when he spied John coming the other way. Now, even though I usually liked John's ideas, Dave did not. From Dave's perspective, John was always having one hare-brained scheme after another, and those schemes always seemed to end up with Dave working lots of extra hours. So when he saw John at the other end of the hall, he did what he always did. He made a quick U-turn and ran in the other direction.

Dave had almost made it to the corner when he heard John shout out to him.

"Dave, hold on a minute!"

He turned around and braced himself for what he expected to be John's latest stroke of creative, but evil, genius.

"How are things going? Good? Good. Listen, next Thursday, I want to have a half-hour show celebrating the fifteenth anniversary of the Kingdome. In the show I want two things to happen. At the end of the show I want Pete Gross"—he's the radio voice of the Seahawks—"to say *Touchdown Seahawks!* fifteen times. And every hour on the quarter hour, from three fifteen to seven fifteen, I want Linda Cohn standing on top of the Kingdome doing cut-ins to promote the show."

The Kingdome was a 250-foot-tall domed stadium a few blocks from Puget Sound, and the wind could be pretty fierce down at ground level. Who knew what it could be like standing on the apex?

Dave said, "Well, John, Linda is six or seven months' pregnant, there are going to be some issues for her standing on top of the Kingdome for four hours."

John just said, "Work them out," and walked away.

Thankfully, Dave had no intention of "working them out." He knew it wouldn't matter to John that he had found out it would take a stunt double and a helicopter to get the job done, so he just lied and told John the Kingdome wouldn't allow it.

In the end John had to settle for me doing off-camera voice-over for the show. But he did get Pete to close the show by saying, "Touchdown Seahawks! Touchdown Seahawks! Touchdown Seahawks! Touchdown Seahawks! Touchdown Seahawks! Touchdown Seahawks! Touchdown Seahawks! Touchdown Seahawks! Touchdown Seahawks! Touchdown Seahawks! Touchdown Seahawks! Touchdown Seahawks! Touchdown Seahawks! Touchdown Seahawks! Touchdown Seahawks!"—which, despite Pete's talents, may not have been as climactic as John probably thought it was going to be.

About six weeks later I gave birth. As soon they placed my daughter in my arms, it was if someone had flipped a switch in my brain. If you're a mother, you probably know what I'm talking about. All the doubts and worries I had about being a good mom vanished and I was so instantly filled with love for this little baby who had been growing inside of me for nine months, I couldn't imagine anything else ever mattering to me again.

Stew became an instant dad, too. Although he never had any doubt about wanting children, I wasn't sure he understood exactly what he was getting himself into when he decided to have children with me. I worked mostly nights and Stew worked days, so Stew was going to be spending a lot of quality time with Sammy by himself, whether he liked it or not.

That first night in the birthing center, I handed Sammy off to Stew around ten o'clock so I could get some rest. I had been through twelve hours of labor. Not unusual for a first birth, but I was exhausted and didn't wake up until about six the next morning. When I woke up, I found Stew and Sammy lying on the couch together fast asleep with Stew's arms safely wrapped around her. That's when I knew for sure that Stew did know what he was getting himself into.

Sammy was a wonderful baby . . . except that she cried very loudly and all the time. I loved her with all my heart, but by the end of the first week I thought I was going to go crazy. The doctors said she had colic, but anyone who has ever had a colicky baby knows that's just a term doctors use to make you feel better. What it really means is, "We have no idea why your child cries all the time and we don't know how to make her stop. What we do know is that the worst of it is going to last six weeks. So get used to it."

The only time Sammy didn't cry in those first six weeks of her life was when she was two weeks old and we took her to see Roseanne Barr. Roseanne has that calming effect on people, don't you think? My friend Laura, whom I worked with at ABC, was working for Roseanne at the time, and she got me free tickets to see her perform at the Paramount Theatre. I felt Sammy was too young to leave with a babysitter, so I just took her with us.

Through two hours of raucous laughter and then half an hour backstage with Roseanne, Sammy slept. On the way back to the car, we marveled at how good she had been, but as soon as we strapped her into her car seat for the ride home she started wailing and didn't stop until three in the morning.

After six weeks, just like the doctor said, Sammy's demeanor improved from crying all the time to just crying most of the time, and we all settled into a routine. I would wake up early with Sammy and spend most of the day with her. At about 3:00 p.m. I would drop her off at my friend's house. My friend would watch her until six o'clock, then Stew would pick her up, and the two of them would spend the evening together.

That's how things went for the next year, and it was a blur. We both spent most of our free time with Sammy, but we rarely did it together. We were a team, but it was more of a tag team, working sequentially more so than together.

The following spring Peter called to tell me ESPN was still interested in me. This time around, Stew didn't give me a hard time and, after a few flights back and forth to Bristol, we were leaving our little house with the flowers and the white picket fence, and moving back east to Connecticut.

SIX

Da Da Da! Da Da Da!

In July 1992 I began my career at ESPN filled with a combination of excitement, trepidation, and the feeling that I just might be the luckiest sports fan on the face of the earth.

It would still be a few years before ESPN ascended to the iconoclastic "Worldwide Leader in Sports" that we all know and love today. There was no ESPN2, ESPNEWS, or ESPN Classic, and late at night you could still catch the ever-popular Duckpin Bowling Championships, but that didn't mean almost every sportscaster I knew didn't want a chance to sit behind the *SportsCenter* desk.

There was definitely a certain amount of prestige that went along with working at ESPN. I was almost uncontrollably proud to have become a *SportsCenter* anchor. But the real difference between working at ESPN and landing a sportscaster job just about anywhere else on TV was the difference between doing a sportscast that lasted four minutes and one that lasted half an hour. (In 1992 the longest *SportsCenter* show was thirty minutes long—not the hour we're all used to now.)

With four minutes, you had barely enough time to run down the scores for your viewers and show a couple of highlights. With thirty minutes, you could run down the scores, show all the most important highlights from around the country, give your viewers a peek at the personal side of some of their favorite players, then tie it together and tell them what it all meant. If you're a sports junkie like me, then you know there's no better fix than that. Nonetheless, there was still that little bit of trepidation, thanks to Dan Patrick, Gary Miller, and Sasha Foo.

Sasha had been a colleague of mine back at KIRO. I always liked Sasha, but when she once described a water pipe explosion at a local men's clothing store on the air as a "dry cleaner's wet dream," she endeared herself to me forever.

When I told Sasha I had accepted a job at ESPN, she sat me right down and said we were going to have to call her friend Gary Miller to get the lowdown. Gary was more than happy to speak to me, but he said the best person to speak to for the lowdown at *SportsCenter* was Dan Patrick. Before I knew it, I was speaking to the famous Dan Patrick.

On the phone, or in person, Dan is pretty much the same guy you see on TV: an engaging, self-assured, straight shooter who tells it like it is with just a touch of dry humor. When he got on the phone, Dan first congratulated me and welcomed me to the ESPN family. Then he wished me luck because, as far as he could tell, I was going to need it. According to Dan, and he was just stating the facts, while ESPN had made a dedicated effort to hire women for on-air positions, they didn't usually last long. Even Gayle Gardner, who became a role model for aspiring young women everywhere, including me, when she became the first female sports anchor for a national TV network, worked at ESPN for only three years before seeming to drop off the face of the earth. Any other women who had preceded me at

ESPN by any length of time didn't even have names you would recognize. But I wasn't worried. I had made a career of succeeding despite the doubts of others; I wasn't going to let the failures of some other women put doubt into my own head. Those other women weren't me.

The best way I can describe what it's like to work at ESPN is to say it's like hanging out at a sports bar, but without the alcohol. Imagine going into work every day, sitting down, and, before doing anything else, turning on the TV on your desk to see how your teams are doing. Then imagine that your boss comes knocking on your door. Instead of trying to hide the fact that you're sitting at your desk watching TV, you flip the screen around so your boss can see it too and you start discussing the game. Then picture yourself heading down to the newsroom to start writing your show and, instead of there being just one TV, there are about twenty, including the one on the desk you're now working at, and they all have direct satellite feeds and you can watch any sporting event you want across the country. Then imagine you're surrounded by about fifteen or twenty other rabid sports fans, just like yourself, and each one of them wants to talk to you about what's going on with their favorite teams. And to top it all off, imagine that someone actually pays you to do this. That's pretty much my job.

Another way working at ESPN was like being at a sports bar was that no one really spent too much time considering the needs of women when they designed the place. I can't really blame them since, at the time, Robin Roberts and I were the only two on-air women working out of Bristol, but it sure makes it difficult for a woman to look presentable when there are no makeup artists, no dressing rooms, and not even an outlet in the ladies' room for you to plug your blow dryer into. I had worked in organizations a tenth the size of ESPN that had both makeup artists and dressing rooms, but it just wasn't something that came up at ESPN. What you had, for years, was a bunch of guys sitting around talking about sports. If you made sure each one combed his hair, and gave him a tie, a jacket, and a little pancake makeup so he didn't look washed out on the set, you were done. Nobody really cares what a guy talking about sports on TV looks like, but put a woman up there and it's another story.

The first coanchor I ever worked with at ESPN was Chris Myers. But during those first two years I was all over the place and working with everyone—Mike Tirico, Dan Patrick, Keith Olbermann, Tom Mees, and Bob Ley, to name a few. When I wasn't on the *SportsCenter* set, I was out doing special-interest stories.

You may not remember—or you may not have even been born yet—but before ESPN forever changed the way we looked at sports and athletes, no network had the time or energy to spend on the human aspect of sports. Nowadays we know everything we want to know, and some things we don't want to know, about our favorite athletes, coaches, and teams. Back in the early 1990s, delving into an athlete's personal life was still relatively novel and I wasn't always prepared for what I would discover, especially at the collegiate level.

One of the first stories I worked on for ESPN was an interview of a former gymnast from the University of Georgia. We all know that the rigors of training and the pressure to keep their weight down can sometimes drag gymnasts to the brink of an eating disorder, but Cheryl had become so thin that she wasn't strong enough to hold herself up during her routines. Although she must have been shockingly thin for some time, it was only after she couldn't perform that her coach and family realized she was dangerously anorexic. Cheryl had to permanently retire from gymnastics, but went public with her story to help other people in similar situations.

When I arrived at Cheryl's proper southern home for the interview, I was first met by her mother, Susanne, who served me tea in the parlor. We made small talk for a while and, although I don't think I'm particularly attuned to this type of behavior, I noticed she had a compulsion to keep everything in its proper place. When I reached for the sugar bowl, for example, and returned it to the serving tray, Susanne couldn't resist nudging it over just a quarter of an inch to make sure it was in line with the creamer. I had noticed similar behavior, although I hadn't realized it at the time, when I interviewed one of Cheryl's former coaches earlier in the day.

When Cheryl came into the parlor to meet me, I was so stunned by her appearance that I had to stifle a gasp. "Officially" she was no longer anorexic, but you couldn't tell that by looking at her. She was pencil thin and looked like you could push her over with just one finger. I was honestly amazed that she could stand without any assistance. During the interview I touched upon her battle with anorexia but focused more on the work she was doing to help others in her situation. Her mother told me Cheryl was now on Prozac and that it had probably saved her life. I know that SSRIs like Prozac have helped a lot of people with chemical imbalances, but in Cheryl's case, and considering the pervasiveness of the obsessive-compulsive behavior around her, I had to wonder whether it was curing a legitimate medical problem or simply covering up the effect of her dysfunctional surroundings. Later on in my life, I would face this issue again when it would be suggested by a mental health care professional that I begin taking an SSRI.

Back at home, things were moving along. Even though I had, once again, dragged Stew across the country and deposited him in a geographic location where there were almost no jobs in his field, he managed to find gainful employment after about four months. The housing market in Seattle had dropped and, like a lot of people, it had taken us seven months to sell our cute little house, at a $40,000 loss. ESPN graciously agreed to give me an advance on my salary so we could afford to pay the mortgage on our home in Seattle while we rented a modest raised ranch at the end of a cul-de-sac in a bedroom community thirty minutes from Bristol.

One evening, while I was giving Sammy a bath, I noticed that something seemed to be wrong with her eyes. I yelled for Stew to come into the bathroom, and together we figured out that her left eye had somehow turned in toward her nose and was stuck there. Her right eye could still move freely, but her left one just stayed in place. Thankfully, Sammy was too young to realize anything was wrong and had simply adapted to her situation by, to put it bluntly, looking at everything out of the side of her face. Later that night, as we sat together reading a good-night story, I hid my tears while I watched her strain her head all the way to the left so she could focus her vision on the pictures in the book.

In high school wearing, of all things, a
NY Islander Jersey

Team Picture: Just giggling away (first row, center, with goalie pads on)

Nothing like a mascot to lift your spirits (Albuquerque Isotoptes' Orbit)

Stoked for my first X Games.
Photo courtesy of ESPN.

Why is Stuart Scott interviewing Chris Berman? I don't know.
Photo courtesy of ESPN.

With Shaun White after he asked me to the prom.
Photo courtesy of ESPN.

A tender moment
with my boss.
**Photo courtesy of
ESPN.**

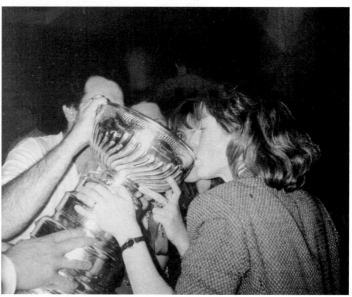

Drinking from the Stanley Cup

Being inducted into the SUNY Oswego Sports Hall of Fame
with my former coach, Rich Tremblay, and my teammates
Anne Potter and Terry Baum

Shea Stadium, 2006 NLCS, Game 7, before the letdown

This stand-up didn't get me in trouble.
Photo courtesy of ESPN.

Making decisions is always difficult. (Note: I'm holding the goalie mask I wore in high school… on the ice.)

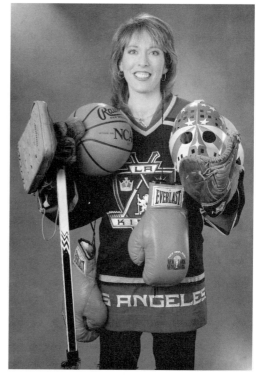

At Super Bowl XL with Emmitt Smith and Darren Woodson.
Photo courtesy of ESPN.

With actor Jason Biggs, before we ate pie

Rocking out with REO
Speedwagon's Dave
Amato. **Photo courtesy of
Bob Critser.**

With my WNBA buddies, Hall of Famer Nancy Lieberman and WNBA
star Becky Hammon. **Photo courtesy of ESPN.**

The next day I brought Sammy to our family doctor, who immediately referred us to a specialist, who in turn referred us to an extra-special specialist. When I called this supposed extra-special specialist on the phone to make an appointment, he told me that he wouldn't be able to see Sammy for a couple of weeks, but not to worry because there would be no further damage to Sammy's eye. He also mentioned, almost casually, that he was familiar with cases of this sort and that he would likely have to sever one or more of the muscles in her left eye to free it from its locked position. I didn't like the sound of that, but I wanted to wait to hear what Stew had to say.

When I told him, he completely blew up. "What does he mean there isn't going to be any further damage? Our daughter's looking out the side of her face and he says there won't be any further damage? How does he know? He hasn't even seen her. And I'll tell you another thing. No one's going to sever anything until we've explored all our other options. You know, there's a sweet little girl in Sammy's day care who had an operation like that, and now she has these thick corrective glasses and she can barely see."

Whoa. That thing about the thick glasses really struck a nerve with me. I knew that pain firsthand and I certainly didn't want Sammy to have to go through it, or something worse.

"What are we going to do?" I asked.

Then Stew said something that made me realize I had underestimated him, again. "Why don't you call your brother and see if he knows any good chiropractors in our area."

What? I couldn't believe Stew was recommending we see a chiropractor. Apparently, unbeknownst to me, Stew and my brother, Howie, had been discussing chiropractic for years. I realized that Stew was a skeptic, but that didn't mean he wasn't interested in what Howie was doing. The two of them had known each other since Howie was in high school and they were, after all, family to each other.

Among the cases they had discussed was one in which Howie had seen a five-year-old boy who couldn't talk, although he seemed reasonably bright in all other respects. The parents had taken him to every conventional medical practitioner they could find until, out of desperation, they took him to see my brother. Howie diagnosed the problem as muscle related and treated the little boy; within a year he was speaking normally. Many people, including me at the time, thought of chiropractors as back people, but Stew figured that if a chiropractor could treat a tongue he could probably treat an eye too.

I called Howie. He knew of an applied kinesiologist—a specialty within chiropractic—not far from where we lived. We took Sammy to see Dr. Robert Porzio, and this is basically what he said:

"The problem is not with Sammy's eye muscles, but with the nerve pathways to those muscles. What probably happened was that Sammy had some sort of physical trauma that disrupted the nerve pathway. At her age it could have been something as seemingly minor as falling on her butt the wrong way. The important thing to understand is that it's not that the muscles on the inside of her eye are pulling too hard, it's that the muscles on the outside of her eye aren't pulling hard enough. That's because they're not receiving the message from her brain to pull. If you severed the muscles on the inside of her eye, you would be cutting the good muscles to compensate for the weak ones. What we need to do is clear the nerve pathway so that the outer muscles begin to get the message from the brain to work again."

To cut right to the chase, we never ended up going to the "extra-special specialist." Instead, with a combination of treatments from Dr. Porzio and Dr. Burke, a nearby vision therapist, along with at-home exercises intended to stimulate her sympathetic nervous system and, of course, a final adjustment from Howie, her eyes were back to normal in about six months.

In the meantime, while all this was going on, I almost got fired from ESPN.

When I was first hired, they offered me a two-year contract with an option for an additional year. This meant ESPN and I had actually negotiated a three-year deal, but the network had the option of dumping me after two years if they didn't like me. It's not really fair, but it is a pretty standard practice. The presumption is that, unless you do something unforgivable, your option will be picked up.

I had been in similar situations before, and I knew there was nothing to worry about. When I worked at ABC Radio, I had an even worse deal where the company had the option of dropping me after every thirteen-week cycle. That, of course, never happened.

Still, somewhere in the back of my mind, I had a lingering doubt. This was compounded by the fact that ESPN never gave me any feedback, good or bad, about how I was doing. I never knew if they were happy with my performance or not, so I worried.

Stew always thought I was being ridiculous. He reasoned that if ESPN was unhappy, they'd tell me because they wouldn't want me trashing up the airwaves. "Besides," he used to say, "you have one of the only jobs where your employers knew exactly how you were going to perform on the job before they hired you because all they had to do was tune in to KIRO on the satellite." As usual, what Stew said seemed to make a lot of sense, even though we would soon find out he was utterly and completely wrong.

But on that fateful day, the last thing I was thinking about was getting fired. It was the spring of 1994, and my Rangers were on their way to winning their first Stanley Cup in more than fifty years. I was doing the six o'clock *SportsCenter* that night, and I was looking forward to getting home early so I could watch the Rangers and Devils battle it out in Game 7 of the Eastern Conference Finals.

When I first got into the studio that day, Steve Anderson and John Walsh, two of my many bosses, told me they wanted me to stop by after the show. My first impression, as always, was that something must be wrong, but after letting Stew allay my fears on the phone, I decided they probably just wanted to talk to me about a special assignment or something.

That night I did the show with Charlie Steiner—if you remember, I used to fill in for him at ABC—and the producer gave me the job at the end of the show to promote the upcoming playoff game between the Rangers and the Devils. "Coming up next, Game 7, Eastern Conference Finals, Rangers, Devils. The winner goes to the Stanley Cup final! It's going to be a classic."

Just doing the promo got me psyched. I couldn't wait to go home. It was about 6:45 p.m. now, and the game started at 7:30.

I figured if my meeting with Steve and John was short, I could be in my car just after 7:00 and home in front of my TV in time to catch the opening face-off.

But things were not to go as expected. I entered the meeting with a broad smile on my face, anticipating the upcoming victory by the Rangers later that night. John and Steve were cordial, but I noticed neither one of them was smiling. I sat down, and Steve went right into it:

"Linda, you've been here for two years now and, well, we thought you'd be making more progress by this time. We know you know sports; that's why we hired you. We can hear it in the newsroom when you talk with your colleagues, but we don't hear that Linda personality when you're on *SportsCenter.* You know we have an option in your contract for another year, and we're not going to pick it up."

Steve went on to tell me they were going to let me stay on without a contract, and without a pay raise, to give me a chance to improve. Then, after a year, we would have another meeting and they would tell me whether or not they were going to offer me a new deal.

I felt like someone had hit me in the face with a baseball bat. I had spent my whole career putting myself in a position to succeed; now it looked like I was perfectly positioned to fail. How was I supposed to excel at my job with a vote of no confidence looming over my head every day?

To a large extent, my career was my life. It defined who I was. Now someone was telling me, in effect, *It may be your life, but, you know what? We don't think you're very good at it.*

I went back to my desk and cried over the phone to Stew until I was able to compose myself enough to drive home. There

I went down to the family room by myself, turned on the TV, and lost myself in the magnitude of an improbable Rangers victory against their "cross-town" rivals, the New Jersey Devils. I watched as Stephane Matteau's double-overtime, wraparound goal propelled my team into the Stanley Cup finals for the first time in fifteen years! Although I didn't hear it until reliving the moment while watching game highlights on TV later that night, Howie Rose's* victory chant of "Matteau! Matteau! Matteau!" will live in my memory forever. After I got my fill of Ranger-induced euphoria, I went right to bed and lost myself in sleep.

The next morning things started looking a little better. Steve had said they were going to hook me up with media coach Andrea Kirby over the next year, so I knew they were at least giving me a fighting chance to pull myself out of this quagmire. Instead of looking at the situation as a disaster, I started looking at it as a challenge, and, win or lose, I almost always rise to a challenge. Besides, I still had to wake up every day and do my job, and I knew I couldn't do that if I felt like I was no good.

Things seemed to improve quickly. Andrea was a big help, bolstering my belief in myself and helping me tweak my on-air performance. Within a few weeks the still-real possibility of being dumped by ESPN was little more than an uncomfortable and nagging worry in the back of my mind. It was still there, but I could usually push it aside, confident now that I would be able to give ESPN what they wanted.

Which was good. Because the hockey season wasn't yet over and I had to be in the right state of mind to watch my Rangers compete against the Canucks for the Stanley Cup. As much as it baffles me, I recognize that not everyone reading this book will be as big a hockey fan as I am. So I'm not going to bore the

---

* Back then, the radio voice of the Rangers. Now he does play-by-play for the Islanders, among other things.

unenlightened with a play-by-play account of how the Rangers took its fans from the fringe of ecstasy, to the depths of despair, and back up through the roof as they alternately won three of four games against the Canucks, lost the next two, and then triumphed in the final and seventh game at home in the Garden. No, I wouldn't do that.

What I do want to tell you about is how I got to drink from the Stanley Cup. After driving home from the devastating Game 5 loss at the Garden, listening to Steve Somers on the radio taking calls from despondent Rangers fans all over the city, and then suffering through one more gut-wrenching loss on the road, I knew, for better or worse, I was going to have to get into the Garden to see the final game of the playoffs. Even though the game was completely sold out.

You're probably thinking, *So what. You're Linda Cohn. You can go to any game at any time.* But it wasn't quite as simple as that. When you spend most of your time in the studio or interviewing anorexic gymnasts, all of which I loved doing, you don't make the same contacts you do when working the beat. Also, keep in mind that this was happening during the aftermath of my vote of no confidence. Personally, I had already moved on, but I wasn't so sure where everyone else was. Obviously, I never mentioned my meeting with Steve and John to anyone else at the station. But I had no idea who knew about it, or whether it affected people's opinions of me, or whether anyone was interested in doing me a favor.

Still, I had to see that game.

I also knew that, being one of the biggest Rangers games ever, there were probably no tickets available, even for people who *hadn't* almost just gotten fired from ESPN. Lucky for me,

ESPN was carrying the Stanley Cup playoffs that year and I was friendly with Mark Quinzel, who was in charge of running remote coverage of the game. I remember walking into his office and pleading my case. I didn't know whether I had any influence or not, but I begged for him to get me in. I said I would do anything. I told him I would bring Gary Thorne, the play-by-play announcer, his coffee. I would bring Bill Clement, the color commentator, a throat lozenge, and I was serious. Whatever it took, I just had to be in that building. Mark understood. He gave me a press pass, and I drove down to the game and found a seat in the press box, sitting with colleagues who may or may not have known that I had almost gotten fired just a few weeks before.

The only problem with sitting in the press box was that I had to behave like a working reporter and not root for my team. It was a tumultuous game, but, like a good girl, I sat on my hands and bit my lip every time I wanted to yell out. In the final minute the Rangers were clinging to a 3–2 lead. The Canucks pulled their goalie for an extra attacker to bolster their offense in an attempt to tie the game and force overtime. Then the Rangers gained possession and took a shot from their end at the open net. The puck sailed across the ice, missing the net and forcing icing to be called. With 1.3 seconds left on the clock, the puck was brought back for a face-off in the Rangers' zone. That may not sound like a lot of time, but to Rangers fans, who have seen the most unlikely events dash their hopes for victory time and again since last winning the Cup in 1940, the threat of losing it all in less than two seconds wasn't only real, it seemed probable.

Luck was with us this time. The ref dropped the puck, the Rangers won the face-off, and the game was over. The press box was in an open area on the top level of the Garden where all the hard-core fans sat (the blue seats). When the final buzzer went off, I couldn't sit on my hands any longer. I jumped up with all the other fans and we were high-fiving and hugging like we were all part of the same family, which we were.

Then I went up to the booth where Gary and Bill had been announcing the game. They congratulated me as if I had been on the ice myself playing the game. I sure felt like I had. I asked if I could use the phone to call my dad, who was at home watching the game on TV. Hank was so happy when I called him, and I could tell over the phone he had been crying tears of happiness, as was I. He said he never thought he would live to see the Rangers win again, and we shared a father/daughter/Rangers moment like no other.

After that emotional phone call, I went down to the locker room area. Since I had a press pass, I would have been able to get into the locker room and celebrate with the team, but I didn't: My rule was that if I wasn't working, I wouldn't go into the locker room. The celebration was spilling out anyway, so it didn't really matter.

During the celebration, I ran into my friend Jeorgi. She was a close friend of Bruce Beck's, who worked for the MSG Network at the time, and he had told her the Rangers would be having their victory party at the Paramount Theatre. We headed down to the Paramount and, as luck would have it, Bruce was right out front when we got there. Bruce and I knew each other well enough for him to know what a big Rangers fan I was, and he got me into the party. Inside was one of the wildest celebrations I've ever experienced. Everybody was carrying on like a terrible curse had been lifted. Then, all of a sudden, out of the corner of my eye I saw the Cup, filled with champagne, and it was calling to me. It was also surrounded by velvet ropes and police officers. Two guys were holding the Cup so people could drink from it. Almost in a trance, and with nothing to lose, I made way over to the ropes. As I approached, one of New York's finest recognized me and, without having to say a word, let me under the rope. Then I walked up to the Cup and, as I was drinking from it, a photographer took my picture. I walked out from behind the ropes, just a couple of months after being told I might not be working at ESPN in a year, and I thought to myself, *Miracles can happen. If they can happen to the Rangers, maybe they can happen to me.*

SEVEN

Growing Pains

One of the things they tell you when you start at ESPN is to think of what you do as "infotainment." That is, you want to "inform" the viewer, but do it in an "entertaining" way. As my friend Keith Olbermann has said, what you have to learn on your own is that, usually, less is more.

Coming from a background, as all of us did back then, where you have four minutes to deliver a sportscast at the end of a local news show, you "grow up" trying to make an impact with everything you say. So when all of a sudden, you're faced with the opportunity to talk about sports for thirty minutes, there's a tendency to want to give the viewer a piece of compelling information delivered with a taste of sarcastic wit in every breath. The irony is, too much wit and information can be worse than too little.

That, I think, is where the burning desire to add catchphrases to our *SportsCenter* broadcasts first arose, and the first catchphrase I remember being uttered by any *SportsCenter* anchor was *En Fuego* by Dan Patrick. (Actually, the first time he used it, Dan said *El Fuego,* which means "the fire", but it quickly evolved to *En Fuego,* or "on fire.") After I heard Dan say that a few times, I thought, *Hey, I want my own catchphrase.* The only problem is, if you purposely try to think up a catchphrase, all you come up with is garbage. I probably should have left it alone, but this was during my year of limbo, after I had almost gotten fired, and I felt I needed to do everything I possibly could to show management I was ESPN material.

So one night I was doing the 11:00 p.m. "Big Show" with Dan, and as I was finishing up a baseball highlight, the incredibly stupid idea of using Dan's catchphrase popped into my head. I don't know what I was thinking, but, apparently I wasn't think-ing much at all because, instead of saying "He's En Fuego!" or even "He's El Fuego!" I stumbled through my delivery and said, very awkwardly, "He's El Frego." *Frego* isn't even a word, either in Spanish or in English! As I finished my fumbled delivery, the camera mercilessly pulled back for a "two-shot" to show Dan just looking at me in disbelief and with an uncomfortable smile on his face.

I've said plenty of stupid things, on and off the air in my career, but that was one of the stupidest, because I not only embarrassed myself, I embarrassed Dan, who, at least before that stunt, had considered me a trusted coworker. As nice as Dan is, he never made mention of the incident.

If you're wondering what other stupid things I've said at ESPN, here are just a couple:

Some years ago I was with the family visiting my friend Susie, who's a freelance graphics coordinator based in Chapel Hill, North Carolina. One afternoon we all loaded up into a cou-ple of cars and drove off to watch Susie pitch for her softball team, the Master Batters.

When I saw the name of the team on the back of her uni-form, I knew I had found a new catchphrase and started using it over baseball highlights. I tried to keep it under the radar by using it sparingly, but I couldn't help myself. In one week I used it to describe both Mike Piazza and Mark McGwire. That's probably what caused *Sports Illustrated* to put a line in one of their columns that said something like, "Did you notice ESPN *SportsCenter* anchor Linda Cohn referring to some members of Major League Baseball as Master Batters?"

That's when Norby, my boss, called me into his office and said, "What are you doing with Master Batter?"

"What?" I said. When I realized that wasn't going to fly, I added, "I was just trying to have a few laughs. I just thought it was a little innocent fun."

"It's not innocent and it's not funny. You have to stop." And that was the end of Master Batting.

Another time, during my year of limbo, we were all in the newsroom discussing a dress code memo we had received from management. Apparently some people had been coming to work dressed just a little too casually, and ESPN wanted to bring things back in line. The memo said something like this:

"As part of the dress code, no employee will be allowed to wear shorts, shirts with team logos, tank tops, or thongs."

It was a pretty straightforward memo, but it left me confused. Sometimes when I'm confused, I keep my mouth shut and wait until the answer comes to me. Other times I just blurt out whatever's on my mind and usually embarrass myself. In this case I was confused and a little annoyed that ESPN would have the nerve to tell me what to wear. I could see not wearing shorts, but I felt it was my business whether I wore a thong or not. So I spoke before thinking too hard about it.

"No thongs? What do they mean? They can't tell us not to wear a thong. How would they know anyway?"

To which one of the men in the newsroom replied. "Oh, we would know, Linda. We would know."

Everyone laughed at the exchange, but I still wasn't sure what was going on. Then someone sitting next to me leaned over and whispered, "Linda, when they said 'thongs' they meant 'flip-flop sandals,' not what you're thinking about."

"Oh."

Despite not being able to tell the difference between a thong and a pair of thongs, I managed to survive my year of limbo. As my twelve months were coming to an end, Steve called me back into his office again, this time with a smile on his face. He told me ESPN was very pleased with the improvement I had made over the last year and that he was happy to offer me a contract. It was a new two-year deal with that standard option for a third year, but, after that first contract, they always picked up the option.

Feeling a little more secure in my position at ESPN, I soon decided the time was right to have another child. For whatever it's worth, I became the first pregnant woman to appear behind a *SportsCenter* desk, and I continued working behind that desk until just thirty-six hours before I gave birth to my son, Daniel.

Over the next few years, the pace really started to pick up for me at ESPN. It seemed I was doing all different types of things: *Baseball Tonight, NHL 2Night, RPM Tonight,* the NFL Draft coverage, *Sunday NFL Countdown,* LPGA coverage, ESPN Radio, and a variety of *SportCenter*s, to name a few. In 1997 ESPN even created a onetime stunt, called Lindapalooza, to highlight my "versatility."

In one day I worked from 9:30 a.m. to midnight and . . .

1. Appeared with the Fabulous Sports Babe on ESPN Radio.
2. Filed a commentary for ESPN Radio that was played throughout the day.
3. Performed as the 10:00 a.m. ESPN news anchor.
4. Did a live chat session on *ESPN SportsZone.*
5. Coanchored an afternoon *SportsCenter.*
6. Did a live interview at the ESPN Club in Disney World.
7. Did voice-over promos for ESPN International (in English).
8. Hosted *NHL 2Night.*

Just the same, I always felt like a sportscaster without a home. It seemed to me that everyone else I worked with could be identified with a certain show, even if they did other things as well: Karl Ravech with *Baseball Tonight,* Stuart Scott and Rich Eisen with the 11:00 p.m. *SportsCenter,* Chris Berman with *Sunday NFL Countdown* (among other shows), and Steve Levy with the NHL.

Then, somewhere in the late '90s, Norby asked me if I wanted to be a permanent anchor for the 1:00 a.m. *SportsCenter.* He warned me that it was a difficult shift and that no anchor could be expected to do it for more than two years, but I jumped at the opportunity to have something I could be identified with, even if it meant everything else in my life had to change.

I worked five nights a week, including every Friday, Saturday, and Sunday, and usually didn't get home until four in the morning. This meant that, on a typical weekday, after a few hours' sleep, I would wake up with the kids, spend a little quality time with them, get them to school and/or day care, do some errands, and then take an hour nap before getting ready to head off to Bristol.

Even though I was doing what I thought was best, I was racked with guilt because I felt like I wasn't spending enough time with my kids. To make things worse for me, a few months later Stew quit his regular job and opened up a small marketing research business out of the house. I fully supported the move and had encouraged him to do it, but now the kids were seeing more of their father than they were of me. My guilt level went through the roof. Stew assured me that I wasn't a bad mother and that, as a team, we were doing what was best for our children. I knew he was right, but that didn't relieve my guilt.

A few weeks passed and I wasn't feeling any better. Then one night, I called from work to talk to my family before they went to bed, as I did every night, and I was greeted by the three of them serenading me.

After listening to me endlessly talk about how guilty I felt about not being there at night with the kids, Stew had written a song to try to make me feel better. It was sung to the tune of Pearl Jam's rendition of "Last Kiss" and inspired by a Saturday morning he had spent with the kids waiting for me to wake up so we could have breakfast together. I didn't know if it was any good, and the beat seemed off at the end, but it absolutely cheered me up and made me see that everything was going to be okay. Here's how it goes:

(Refrain)
Oh where, oh where can my Mommy be?
She got home late.
She's tired as can be.
But now its mornin'.
And though she looks so sweet
I hope she gets up soon.
So we can eat.

My mom works late
Almost every night
I don't like it
But she is quite a sight

She gets on the TV
They all know her name
They can't wait
To hear about the game

She talks about the sports
She smiles and jokes
About Randy Moss
And how the Rangers choked

She loves it so much
She can't get enough
But I'm at home

And my Dad is tough

Refrain

My mom loves us so
Of that I'm really sure
She gives us hugs and kisses
And so much more

But late at night
When no one is around
I wish she were at home
I wish she were found

My dad is okay
He isn't too bad
But when he makes meat loaf
I get real sad

I know if my mom
Were home tonight
Then we could have McDonald's
And we'd be all right

Refrain

Well now our story's told
I guess it's not so sad
My life is okay
My room is not half bad

(Sammy)
I got my CDs
And my neighbor Kaitlin
She is kind of weird
But trouble we are makin'

(Daniel)
My life is good too
I like to tease Sammy
I know that it's cruel
But she's the one who taught me

My mom says she'll have weekends off
It won't be too long
But until that day
I'll sing this song.

Refrain

Ooooh ooooh ooooooh . . .

EIGHT

A Day in the Life

Here's what a typical day doing the 1:00 a.m. (ET) *Sports-Center* is like.

Having worked until the wee hours of the morning the night before, I usually try to wake up around 10:00 a.m. In the early days, as I've mentioned, I would wake up with my kids to get them ready. Nowadays their buses come too early for me, so I just let Stew get them ready for school.

The first thing I do when I wake up in the morning is throw some clothes on and run out to get a cup of coffee and a plain bagel, nothing on it. Call me a coffee snob, but I just don't like home-brewed coffee. So after working until 4:00 a.m., or later, the night before, the very first thing I have to do in the morning is get a good cup of coffee.

Bleary eyed and with my hair pulled back in a loose pony-tail, the one thing I can be sure of is that the worse I look in the morning, the more likely I am to run into a fan. Another thing I can be pretty sure of at that time of morning is that the fan, whether it's a man or a woman, will say, "You're so much better looking in person than you are on TV!" I find it amazing that anyone can even recognize me looking like the way I do in the morning, so when they tell me I look better in person, without even a shower, it makes me wonder just how bad I really looked on the air the night before.

After my coffee, I do before work what most other moms do after work. On any given day, I'm usually about three loads behind in the laundry, so I go back home, throw a load in, and read the sports section of the *New York Post* before I head out and run whatever errands I need to on that day. Our house is always cluttered, so when I come home from my errands, I try, with varied success, to straighten up some part of the house. In the early afternoon I take a nap, work out, take a shower, and then head off to Bristol in time to get there for the 6:00 p.m. Rundown Meeting.

At the meeting, seven hours before the red light goes on, are the producer, the director, the coordinating producer, the associate producer, my coanchor, and me. This first meeting is very informal; we basically sit around a table talking about where the big stories are, where our reporters are, and how much coverage we want to give to each story or game.

We talk through the stories and share our individual knowledge and perspectives to see if there's something hidden there that we can bring out. Maybe there's a player who's been overlooked but deserves to be recognized for his achievements. Or perhaps there's a background or personal story about a player's off-the-field life that explains or enhances what's happening on the field.

We also, usually, wrestle with how much time we devote to the stories that always seem to be there, but probably receive a little too much coverage. It seems like there's always a story we can do on the Yankees or Red Sox, but do we want to do another Yankees story just because it's easy? There's also the dilemma of what we do with stories about Barry Bonds, Terrell Owens, and other guys who are making news for the wrong reasons. We know viewers want to know what's going on with these players, but there's a fine line between giving these stories adequate coverage and celebrating bad behavior.

Here's an example of everything I've just been talking about, all wrapped up in one story. As I'm writing this, Barry Bonds is approaching the point where he is going to be breaking Hank Aaron's home run record—something we never thought we'd see. This is phenomenal baseball history. At a Rundown Meeting, Bonds is only seven away from breaking the record and we're talking about how we need to start stepping up our coverage of this incredible piece of baseball history.

But then, well, wait a minute—because of the whole steroid cloud surrounding Bonds, not even Major League Baseball is making a big deal out of it. Do we celebrate bad behavior? Also, over the years, Bonds's outspoken comments on just about everything have made him a lot of enemies, to the point where almost no one outside of San Francisco likes him or probably cares what he does.

Then we start speculating. Can you imagine if Bonds is one away from the record and he's about to enter an eight-game road trip? He's not going to want to break the record on the road. At best, he'll get a lukewarm response. So then what happens? If Bonds goes through eight away games without even trying for a home run, he'll be booed everywhere he goes. What will he do?

Then Ira Fritz, the guy who writes our tease bumps, says "I'll tell you what's going to happen. Bonds is going to fake some injury—shin splints, or that nagging knee injury, or something else. He'll do whatever he can to avoid the thought of breaking this record on the road."

If Fritzy is right, that could be really intriguing TV. If we come out and predict this now, it could be a feather in our cap. But if we're wrong, then we'll have to eat our words. There might be a great story in there, but there's just too much that is unknown. We'll have to wait, but be poised to pick it up later if it all comes together.*

Following the meeting, the producer and coordinating producer put together the rundown. That's when I usually go upstairs to my office, turn on sports radio, check my e-mails, and try to get up to speed on all of the big stories for the night. Even though I don't yet know what stories I'll be doing, I need to know about everything that's going on because, first and foremost, I'm still a sports fan and I just need to know. But I also need to be fully informed on what's going on so that I can do my job right. On *SportsCenter* you can't just go through the show knowing your little part of it. You have to know everything that's going on so you can interact with your coanchor and also pick up a late-breaking story if one pops up during the show.

About an hour after the meeting, the producer posts the rundown on the computer network and I look through it to see what stories I'll be doing. Even though we try to be impartial on the air, the producer knows where our passions lie and tries to give each of us the stories we're most interested in. I can't always get the stories I want, but, on any given day, if there's a

---

* After going twenty-eight at-bats without a home run, Bonds tied Hank Aaron's record in San Diego on August 4th. On August 5th he chose to celebrate with his family rather than play another game away in San Diego. On August 7th, he broke the record at home against Mike Bacsik of the Washington Nationals. You make the call.

story about one of my favorite teams or players, there's a good chance I'm going to get to do it.

After looking to see which stories I'll be doing, I scan the rundown to see how many on-camera lead-ins I've got. In other words, the big question is: How many times am I introducing a story by talking behind a highlight or a scoreboard, and how many times am I face-to-face with the viewer? Some people misconstrue this interest in on-camera lead-ins as nothing more than ego, but that's not really it. Sure, I want my face to be seen on TV—otherwise I'd be on radio—but what it's really all about for me is a way to visually, as well as verbally, communicate with the viewer. Face time also allows me to show off my writing skills, because an on-camera lead-in always gives you more time to set up the story and add something the viewer didn't know.

Once the rundown comes in, we all go down to the pod. The pod is a relatively recent innovation that we all hated when it was first introduced, but now love. Before the pod, it was common practice for the anchors to get the rundown and then hole themselves up in their offices to write their shows. It made sense to me and pretty much everyone else. Writing for *SportsCenter* is an intense process that requires a high level of concentration. Being able to sit in the peace and quiet of your office, with the door closed and no one to interrupt you, was, I thought, critical to putting out a quality show.

Mark Shapiro, the executive vice president of programming at the time, one day changed all that. He made a new rule that all the anchors had to write their shows down in the newsroom, where there is all kinds of noise and a constant barrage of interruptions. I thought he was crazy, so I did what I usually do in situations like this. I ignored him and just kept going up to my office to write the show.

I wasn't the only one, and we all thought this whole crazy idea would blow over in a week or two. While the success of ESPN has been built on many things, the one thing holding it altogether—thanks largely to John Walsh, the executive editor of ESPN since 1990—is its emphasis on writing quality. How were we supposed to maintain that high level of writing while immersed in the cacophony of the newsroom?

But the whole thing didn't blow over. After a couple of weeks of discreetly ascending to my office to write the show, I was "spoken to" and told that I absolutely had to go down to the pod.

The word *pod* doesn't exactly elicit images of a sophisticated writing environment, and I can tell you that it actually looks even less impressive than it sounds. Essentially, the pod is a group of four desks, situated amid a sea of other desks in the middle of the newsroom, all facing one another. Sitting at the four desks are the two anchors for the show, the producer, and the coordinating producer. The premise behind the pod is that it's designed to promote team chemistry and increase the quality of the show. Remarkably, it does. Facing the three other people you rely on most to get the show on the air, you can't help but discuss story issues, debate different points of view, analyze and reanalyze coach or manager decisions, and ruminate over the long-term impact of athlete controversies on and off the field. It's an amazingly synergistic and creative environment that truly leads to a more incisive show. As with any creative process, it also leads to a lot of spillover.

When I first started coanchoring *SportsCenter*, I wondered why I needed to come in seven hours before the show to write my half of a thirty-minute show that also included outside reports and commercials. But I realized, once I started doing it, that while it doesn't take seven hours of continuous, nose-to-the-grindstone work to get the show on the air, it does take pretty close to that amount of time to plan the show, make changes to it as things change in the field, and mold and synthesize it into something that's worth watching.

On any given day, then, there's a good amount of downtime when you're either waiting for games to finish or need a break so you can divert your attention from the task at hand and mull it over in your head. As much as anything, it's this need for diversion that has led to what I call the Bristol Games. These are games or contests created by various people at ESPN designed to kill time while you're waiting for a game to end and also break the tension of putting together a show that always has last-minute changes:

Guess the Crappy NBA Game

If you're an NBA fan, you know what I'm talking about. Basketball is an exciting sport, but no matter what teams you're watching, you just never know when you're going to tune into one of the most boring games of the season. Guess the Crappy NBA Game came out of an effort to vent our frustration.

Here's how the game works. Someone will come over and say, "Guess the score." Then they'll rattle off three possible scores for a crappy NBA game and you have to guess which one is real.

For instance: "Guess the score: Spurs versus Cavs. Is it 82 to 70 with forty-five seconds left in the game, 60 to 54 in the third quarter, or 36 to 29 in the second half?"

Stump the Pod

This is a pure TV trivia game that has nothing to do with sports. It was originated by my coordinating producer, Gus Ramsey.

What usually happens is that Gus will ask a meaningless trivia question that you know just enough about so that it nags on your brain until you find out the answer. Once, he asked, "What are the one hundred most memorable characters on TV of all time?" Another time we had to name all the people in the "We Are the World" video.

Umpire: Dead or Alive

This one was created by Jud Burch, one of our coordinating producers. I think it's self-explanatory, but just in case it's not, the object of the game is to decide whether a certain umpire is dead or alive. It's not that we don't like umpires, most of the time. It just gives us something to do.

Name the Fake School

The brainchild of Jud Burch and producer Scott Clark, this is a game based on college basketball.

Every week, during the season, Jud will pass around a list of final scores for about twenty Division 2 and 3 teams. You have to guess which school doesn't exist. It's not as easy as you'd think. Here's an example:

Sandellion 47, Steamboat 39

Immaculata 64, Arcadia 62

Crown 60, Trinity Bible 54

Maine-Farmington 76, Thomas 58

Mary Washington 73, Marymount 64

NC Wesleyan 114, Roanoke 56

North Park 65, Robert Morris-Springfield 64

Arkansas Tech 82, Crichton (Tenn.) 76

Metropolitan State College of Denver 92, St. Francis (Ill.) 73

Albertson 111, Evergreen 87

West Virginia 81, Connecticut 71

Mineral Area 69, Highland 57

Eulanvita 60, Folara 58

Okaloosa-Walton 101, Georgia Perimeter 100 OT

Benedict 81, Lincoln Memorial 68

Paine 70, Lane 66

Alderson-Broaddus 116, Penn State-New Kensington 34

Risper Methodist 43, Mooney 42

There are three fake games. To find out, look at the bottom of the page.

The fake games are: Sandellion 47, Steamboat 39; Eulanvita 60, Folara 58; Risper Methodist 43, Mooney 42.

Umpire Fantasy League

Jud, admittedly, is obsessed with umpires. It's because as a kid he loved baseball but couldn't play to save his life. To get close to the game, he became a Little League umpire. I don't know anyone else who's really that interested in umpires (no offense, Jud), but this game is so popular that it's even been mentioned, surreptitiously, on *SportsCenter*.

It works similarly to a baseball fantasy league, only with umpires, and it's a lot easier to keep score. In the league, there are twelve teams, and each team is randomly assigned two of the twenty-four lead umpires. You score a point every time your umpire ejects somebody from a game.

Tim Kirkjian says, "This is the single stupidest exercise I've ever been a part of, but I love it."

The teams have names like The Blue Man Group, The Plate Coats, Ump Up the Volume, and Brock & Chest Protector. If you're a faithful and astute watcher of *SportsCenter*, you just might have noticed an obtuse remark here and there that didn't seem to make any sense: "That's one for The Blue Man Group" or "Tim Cheetah, that's a point for me." Now you know what they mean.

Actually, the inclusion of inside jokes into *SportsCenter* broadcasts is a long-standing tradition that began in the early '90s with the master, Keith Olbermann. But even with Keith long gone on to other adventures, the inside jokes continue. The reason for this, as I said earlier, is because working at ESPN is like hanging out at a sports bar. Sure, there's a lot of hard work to be done, but we're all having a blast doing it, and when the cameras go on, everything we've been doing for the last seven hours—the keeping track of scores, the analyses, the sports discussions, and the game playing—all overflows into the show.

One day in the spring of '07, Jud comes up to me before a show and says, "Name the first and last number one songs of the '70's." I think I can get this one, but I ask him to give me a little time to figure it out. While we're on our way to the set, Jud gives me a hint: There's a liquid in both songs.

So even though I'm going on the air in just a few minutes, I'm thinking about '70s songs that have liquids in them. I start thinking about Creedence Clearwater Revival—they've got a couple of rain songs: "Have You Ever Seen the Rain?" and "Who'll Stop the Rain." It's the right time frame, but I don't think either one of those made number one. I keep thinking.

Now I'm on the set with my , John Anderson, and I'm getting all my stuff together for the broadcast. Then I hear Jud in my earpiece: "The first one is a soundtrack. Remember, it's 1970 and the world was a kinder place." That's all the hint I need. I press the button on my mike so that Jud can hear me, and I say, "'Raindrops Keep Fallin' on My Head,' sung by B. J. Thomas, and it was in the movie *Butch Cassidy and the Sundance Kid.*"

But I'm still having trouble with the last number one hit of the '70s. All through the show I'm trying to think of that last song, but I just can't come up with it. John already knows the answer, and he's teasing me relentlessly throughout the show.

I always associate music with things that were happening in my life at the time, so I think to myself, *What else was going on at the end of 1979?* I turn to my default point of reference. *Let's see, the Rangers lost to the Flyers in the quarter finals that year.* But that doesn't really help because the quarter finals didn't happen until a few months into 1980.

I'm totally stumped. The broadcast is wrapping up and I have to throw to the next show. I say something like, "Highlights of the Yankees coming up on *Baseball Tonight.* Don't miss it." Then I pass it over to John to sign us off. The camera pulls back and he says, "Or you could just sit back and have a piña colada." Then I realize the song I've been trying to remember. It's "Escape (The Pina Colada Song)" by Rupert Holmes. We're still in front of the camera but I kind of lose myself in the moment. I have a wide-eyed expression, my mouth is open in surprise, and I blurt out, "Oh! I like that song." Then we go straight to commercial and the show's over.

So the next time you're watching *SportsCenter* and you think one of the anchors has said something extremely witty, you might be right. Or it might just be an obscure reference to something that was going on before the show began.

While we're busy putting the show together, and intermittently relieving tension with things like Stump the Pod and Name the Song, there are a dozen or so production assistants (PAs), the unsung heroes of *SportsCenter,* watching all the different games that are going on. Each PA is assigned to a single game and is in charge of putting a shot sheet together for the game's highlight. The shot sheet is a summary of what's going to happen during the highlight; it's written to tell the story in thirty-five seconds.

Here's an actual copy of a shot sheet for a Michigan State—Illinois game:

SITUATION	ACTION	RESULTS
TRT: 0:46	DREW NEITZEL leading the Spartans into Illinois coming off their 29 point win against Indiana...	
early on, the Spartans looked shaky...	Illinois' DEMETRI MCCAMEY (MC-CAME-EE) misses the jumper...but nobody boxes out RODNEY ALEXANDER...he grabs the rebound and puts it back for two...	...TOM IZZO not happy...ILLINOIS went up by 10 points early
Later in the 1st half...Spartans working the pick and roll...	...NEITZEL gets a pick from DREW NAYMICK, then finds him on the drive for the dunk down low...	...Spartans within 8...game tied at 31 at the half...
2nd Half...Spartans up by 2...	...NAYMICK hits the jumper at the foul line...	...Spartans go up by 4...
NAYMICK even involved for ILLINOIS...	...TRENT MEACHAM throws the inbounds pass off NAYMICK's backside, MEACHAM then catches it for the score...	...Illinois pulls within 4...
Late 2nd half...Spartans up three...	DREW NEITZEL knocks down the three on the catch and shoot	...Spartans go up by 6...

On a rare occasion you'll get a shot sheet and highlight to look at before the show begins. But nine times out of ten, you get the shot sheet on the set during the middle of the show. That's what makes it so exhilarating. When the viewer is seeing the highlight for the first time on TV, I'm often seeing it for the first time as well, keeping one eye on the monitor and the other on the shot sheet as I try to explain to my audience what's going on in real time.

Unlike radio and even old-time TV, where you have your hands in every little bit of the show, a modern *SportsCenter* show, or any other show on ESPN, is a team effort. You really have to trust other people. This is hard for me because, no matter who makes the mistake, it always looks like it's the anchor's fault. In a show like *SportsCenter,* there are about a gazillion mistakes that can be made by other people. A score can be wrong, a statistic can be wrong, a spelling can be wrong, the name of a player can be wrong. It just goes on and on.

If I get a shot sheet or some research material before the show, I can check the facts myself before I go on. But when someone throws a shot sheet on your desk minutes before you're going to read it on the air, there isn't time to even look at it before the words come out of your mouth. Sometimes as I'm about to say something, I realize it's wrong as I'm saying it and I can correct myself. But most times things are happening so quickly, I can't be sure of myself and have to trust what's been written down for me.

And trust is a hard thing for me. You know how they have that psychological test on trusting people where you stand with your eyes closed, cross your arms in front of you, and then fall backward into the arms of someone you're supposed to trust? I can't do that. I couldn't, can't even do that with Stew.

More about that later. Getting back to the show, mistakes are going to happen no matter what. It's just the nature of live TV. No matter how careful people are. No matter how dedicated they are to their jobs, there are going to be screwups.

And when a screwup happens, my knee-jerk reaction, for years, was to come storming off the set at the end of the show and say, "*Who* was responsible for that?" Remember, that's how I grew up. If something went wrong, not just on the set, but with anything, I always wanted someone to blame.

It became such a common mantra of mine that around the pod, my coworkers would joke that ESPN should give me a sports-related game show called *Who's Responsible?* We even developed a little pitch. The show would highlight sports screwups of the week, and I would spend most of the show fingering managers and coaches and players. We even had a sponsor in mind: Planned Parenthood. We thought, what possible sponsor better epitomizes responsibility than Planned Parenthood?

But you know what? I don't want to play that game anymore—and I don't think I have for a long time—because there are no winners in that game. In a best-case scenario, the person I've yelled at thinks I'm a bitch, goes home angry, curses me out, and stops putting their all into their job when I'm anchoring. In the worst-case scenario, I've made someone so afraid of making a mistake that they're bound to make another one.

It's like what they say in NASCAR: If your goal is not to hit the wall, the very best you can expect is not to hit the wall. If don't quite reach your goal, then you will definitely hit the wall. On the other hand, if your goal is to drive the best race you can, you just might come in first; and if you don't quite reach your goal, you might still drive a pretty good race.

That said, there's almost never a *SportsCenter* when something doesn't go wrong. But if we've all tried to do our best, there's a good chance that we can go home happy with the job we've done. Unless we're doing the 1:00 a.m. *SportsCenter.* That's because the 1:00 a.m. show is re-aired every morning from 5:00 a.m. until noon.* As a result, any mistake that's made

---

* ESPN has begun live *SportsCenter* broadcasts starting at 6:00 a.m. EST. The 1:00 a.m. re-airs are now a thing of the past.

during the live broadcast has to be fixed so that we don't look like a bunch of idiots, making the same mistake over and over again for seven hours the next day.

A fix can be anything. Maybe a name or score is wrong on a graphic. Or maybe one of the anchors made a mistake. I've definitely made my share of errors, flubbing a name, missing a cue, whatever. Other times, though, there's a technical error that you don't even know about until the show is over. What can happen is, you and your coanchor will have done a flawless show and you're just about to leave your chairs when you hear in your ear, "There was a problem with a spelling" or "You gave the right score, but it was wrong on the graphic. We're going to have to do that whole segment over again." Then, instead of getting home at 3:00 a.m., you don't get home until 4:00 or 5:00. It's especially fun when there's been a New England blizzard that night and the hill up to your house hasn't been plowed yet.

As luck would have it, Steve Berthiaume and I, along with countless behind-the-scenes personnel, have the distinction of doing the longest non-tragedy-related *SportsCenter* ever. It was the Friday night in 2001 when Barry Bonds broke the single-season home run record. The game was in San Francisco, and we had to go live to every Bonds at-bat so we could be there in case he broke the record. After he broke the record and the game had ended, we went to live coverage of the podium ceremony and the press conference, none of which was going to be re-aired the next morning. When we were finally done, we couldn't just delete those pieces we weren't going to re-air—we had to redo the entire show. At about three o'clock in the morning, instead of being home and crawling into our respective beds, we were rewriting the show. It wasn't until 6:18 a.m. that we finally heard those two magical words—"Studio clear!"—and we all went home. Let me tell you, there's something special about getting home so late that you're just in time to wake up your son for school.

NINE

Rock 'n' Roll

Without a doubt, the very best career I could ever have had was to become a sportscaster. However, in my dreams, if I couldn't be a sportscaster, I would have wanted to be a rock star. If I couldn't have been a rock star, then I would have wanted to be a groupie. Well, the truth is, I already am a groupie, and have been ever since the first time I saw David Cassidy on *The Partridge Family*.

The funny thing is, as much as I'm a hopeless rock groupie, a lot of rockers are groupies of mine. It's not their fault; it's just the fallout from our modern times. While I've always thought of rock 'n' roll as a thrill-packed business filled with screaming fans and all-night partying, what I've discovered is a lot of nights on the road end with these hard-core rockers sitting in tour buses or motel rooms in front of a TV watching *SportsCenter*. I've had more than one musician come up to me somewhere and say, "I go to bed with you every night." Music may be the universal language, but, at least in America, sports come in a close second.

Over the years I've had the privilege of meeting a number of great artists, largely because they're such big sports fans. A few years ago, when I was at a charity event in Colorado held by John Elway, I had stepped outside to get a breath of fresh air when someone called out, "Hey, Linda." I turned around to see Bruce Hall and Dave Amato, the bass player and lead guitarist from REO Speedwagon, one of my favorite bands from my college days. Turns out, they're huge *SportsCenter* fans and, when they were playing in Connecticut a few months later, I invited them up for a tour of ESPN. They, in turn, gave me two tickets to a concert they were doing the following night.

The next thing I know, I'm at the concert with Heather, a cameraperson and fellow huge REO fan, when Dave says, "Hey, later on, make your way backstage and you two can sing back up for us on 'Roll with the Changes.'" (That's my favorite REO song. Even more so than "Time for Me to Fly.") During the song, I share a mike with Dave and Heather shares one with Kevin Cronin, the lead singer. After the concert, the band gives me a copy of my performance on DVD and a pass good for access to every concert they'll perform that year. They must have taken a second look at my singing performance, though, because at the end of the year no one offered to renew my pass. I still have the DVD, but I'm thinking about destroying the evidence.

More recently, after interviewing him for my online hockey column, I've become friendly with John Ondrasick from Five for Fighting. John's a humongous LA Kings fan and, as you might know, the name of his group is a hockey penalty reference.

Of all the musicians I've met, though, one of my all-time favorites has to be Bowling for Soup. As far as I'm concerned, there's something you have to love about a band that takes a bad review—they were once written up as being "the worst pop band in the history of music . . . period!"—and puts it on the back of one of their concert T-shirts as a badge of honor.

I first met the band when I was covering the Summer X Games in 2004. Chris Burney, the lead guitarist, is a hopeless Cowboys fan, and he asked a mutual friend, Jed Drake,* to introduce us at an X Games after-party we were both attending. Two hours later we were still talking about the Cowboys, Texas Rangers, and Dallas Stars. The rest, as they say, is history.

One day as I was writing this book I received a text message from Chris about his Cowboys. Greg, the drum tech for the band, is forever sending me good-natured but antagonistic messages about how his Chiefs are the greatest team in the league and my Giants are going to choke. But as much as it surprises me to say this, it's not the sports connection that I love most about them. It's that this heavily tattooed and pierced band, with a song catalog generously laden with four-letter words and punk/slacker attitude, is one of the nicest, most fun-loving, and humble bunch of guys I have ever met.

Last year, when they invited my family and me backstage at a concert they were playing at Rye Playland, I watched from the rear entrance of the concert hall as they signed autographs in the parking lot. When a group of fans noticed me and started yelling "Linda! Linda!" not only wasn't Bowling for Soup bothered that I might steal some of their thunder, they encouraged me to join them to sign autographs.

As much as I love Bowling for Soup and their road crew, nothing compares to my encounter with my very first heartthrob, David Cassidy. As a young girl, I knew when his birthday was (April 8), where he lived (Laurel Canyon), and what kind of car he drove (I don't remember anymore, but I think it was red). When I was twelve, I talked my mother into letting me take the Long Island Rail Road with my friend, Erin,** into Manhattan to

---

* Senior Vice President and Executive Producer at ESPN
** I guess I had five friends then.

see a David Cassidy concert at Madison Square Garden. Long before I ever saw the Rangers at the Garden, I was up in the cheap seats screaming my head off for David Cassidy.

In 1997 Rich Eisen was set to do a human-interest story in Las Vegas prior to the Evander Holyfield–Michael Moorer fight. It was the first time ESPN was sending him out of the studio to do a piece, and he wanted to really wow them. Rich told me, "I don't want to make this one of those typical X's and O's boxing preview pieces. It's Vegas, so I want to incorporate some of the regular acts on the Strip into the piece to make it funny."

He pulled out some Vegas show flyers and was telling me about the different acts he was going to try to incorporate into the story when I saw a brochure for the MGM Grand with David Cassidy on the cover. Expectedly, I went crazy, and Rich said he would try to incorporate my infatuation with David Cassidy into the piece. Although it's kind of an unwritten law for a reporter not to ask a celebrity for an autograph, I broke the rule and asked Rich if he would *please* get me a signed photograph if at all possible.

Rich developed an outline for the piece he was going to do and, when he approached David Cassidy with the idea, he was surprised to find out that David was actually a fan of mine. He was happy, he said, to go along with Rich's idea. The final piece begins with Rich meeting David in his dressing room and asking him if they can hang out together after the show. David tells Rich that he'd like to, but his favorite *SportsCenter* anchor is Linda Cohn (me!) and he feels it would be like cheating on me if he hung out with Rich. Then the camera pans back to reveal that David's entire dressing room is plastered with pictures of me. I know it was just an amusing, made-up piece, but when I saw David acting as if *he* was infatuated with *me,* I became that twelve-year-old little girl again.

Alas, my fantasy was destroyed a few years later when I was in California for the opening of Disney's California Adventure and I saw David there with a Yankees cap on. *A Yankees cap!* I could have accepted David being a Dodgers fan since they both moved to Los Angeles around the same time, but why did he have to be a Yankees fan? We agreed to stay friends despite our differences.

Hanging out with some of my favorite musicians and talking with them about what their music has meant to me is a dream come true. Talking with John Ondrasik about the inspiration behind songs like "100 Years" and "The Riddle" is like discovering a hidden treasure. But let's face it: Getting a call from one of the hunkiest actors of all time is a whole different kind of thrill.

It all began when I was doing the 11:00 p.m. *SportsCenter* one night and had to get away from the pod for a few minutes. What's especially tension-inducing about the eleven o'clock show is that most of the games you're going to be talking about on the air are still going on, so the rundown, and your writing, are changing minute by minute. Sometimes things get so hectic that you just need to escape upstairs to your office for a little while to catch your breath.

When I got to my office and closed the door, I noticed the light on my phone blinking. Checking the message, I heard, in a home-grown Texas drawl, "Hi, Linda. This is Matthew McConaughey."

His tone was like we were old friends. "Hey, I'm going to be in town next month to host *Saturday Night Live.* My girlfriend is at UCLA and she's very interested in doing what you're doing some-day. I was thinking, if it's okay, I would love to send her out there. Maybe you could spend some time with her and tell her what it's all about."

How do you say no to Matthew McConaughey? Who would even want to? So I gave Matthew's then-girlfriend, Michelle, a tour; afterward we sat down and talked about what it was like to be a woman in sportscasting. I was on my guard at first, because I didn't have high expectations for what type of coed Matthew McConaughey would be dating, but she turned out to be not only attractive, as expected, but also smart, with a clear plan of where she wanted to go in her career.

Soon after, Matthew called me on my cell phone to thank me and we, inevitably, ended up talking about his Texas Long-horns, who were on their way to a national championship. Years later, I finally met him when I interviewed Matthew and his costar, Matthew Fox, while they were promoting the film *We Are Marshall.* I would have thought he'd have other things on his mind, but the first thing he said to me was, "Hey, Linda, I just want to thank you again. I'm not seeing Michelle anymore, but I just want to say thanks for everything you did."

Not every celebrity encounter, however, goes quite so well. For a while, on ESPN, we had this thing called the Budweiser Hot Seat. It was fast-paced interviewing for the new millennium. Conducted via satellite, each interview lasted just a minute and thirty seconds. There was no conversation, no small talk, no leisurely retrospection, just a rapid-fire barrage of tough but good-natured questions, designed to catch the person being interviewed off balance and make for entertaining TV.

As with every new concept they conjured up at ESPN, I wanted to be a part of it. Sure, I was happy doing the 1:00 a.m. *SportsCenter,* but I always wanted more. That's my nature.

Eventually, I got my turn. Bruce Willis and Matthew Perry were reprising their roles of Jimmy and Oz in *The Whole Ten Yards,* and, squeezing into an already jam-packed day of interviews, they agreed to appear with me for ninety seconds on the Hot Seat.

Up until that point, the Hot Seat had only been used to interview athletes, but this was a perfect interview setup for me. Aside from the fact that they were promoting a football movie, I had been a huge Bruce Willis fan ever since his *Moonlighting* days, and Matthew Perry's Chandler had been my favorite character on *Friends.* Matthew, I knew, was also an avid hockey player; my mother and I had even met him once at an earlier ESPY Awards ceremony. This was going to be great. I couldn't wait to show ESPN what I could do in ninety seconds.

I went down to the studio and waited for the satellite feed. Bruce and Matthew had been doing interviews since early that morning and, by the afternoon, they were horribly backed up. I waited in my chair for two hours until they were finally ready to talk to me. I was probably one of the last interviews they were doing that day, which meant they'd already done two more hours of interviewing than they had planned.

Usually when I do an interview, I meet with the person beforehand so we can develop a rapport and go over what we'll be talking about. That's always been my secret to doing a good interview. With the Hot Seat, though, you meet the interviewee as he appears on the screen and you just start asking questions. It's supposed to make the interview more spontaneous and, hopefully, funnier.

When Bruce and Matthew finally came on screen, I could see they were fried from a full day of answering questions and trying to be witty and amusing. The format of the Hot Seat interview is very rigid, so I quickly welcomed them to the Hot Seat and began firing away.

Right from the start, I could see that not only were they fried, but no one had briefed them about the unique setup of the interview. For someone who's never seen the Hot Seat, the questions can seem bizarre, or even rude. I was looking for quick answers, but Matt and Bruce were just easing into the interview and making jokes between themselves. Forty-five seconds went by before they even tried to answer the first question. I kept jumping in trying to regain control of the interview, but they refused to get with the program.

Matt said something like, "Hold on, Linda. We're trying to answer your question. What's your problem?" It seemed like they were angry at me. Matthew was sarcastic and Bruce just seemed annoyed. It's pretty intimidating when it looks like Bruce Willis is angry at you. On top of that, their feed was coming from LA, so there was a three-second delay between the time I said something and the time they heard it, which made the cadence of the interview even more awkward. When the ninety seconds was up, that was it. With the Hot Seat, there are no second takes, no edits; I just had to say good-bye. They were like, "Yeah, thanks a lot, Linda."

When the set was clear, my producer came up to me and said, "I know it wasn't your fault, but that was a disaster. We're going to have to scrap the whole interview." So much for impressing everyone with my skills on the Hot Seat. I never did it again.

The next year I saw Matthew at the ESPY Awards (he was hosting them) and, even though I knew I had to clear the air with him, I was afraid and embarrassed. I asked Pam Litton, who had been in charge of booking guests for the show, to go over to him and feel him out. I could see an animated discussion occurring between the two of them, and then Matthew came over and we cleared up the whole matter. They were just trying to be funny, he said; it was all a misunderstanding. "We're good," he said. One day I hope to get closure with Bruce Willis. Yippee-kay-yay.

My run-in with Joshua Morrow, however, went much better, which is surprising considering he's a Brewers fan (just kidding). How that one began was that John Anderson and I were in the pod for the 1:00 a.m. show with Jud Burch, and I overheard the two of them talking about *The Young and the Restless.* I was only half listening to what they were saying—I had always been more of an *All My Children* fan—but when they mentioned Joshua Morrow, something clicked in my brain.

I said, "Joshua Morrow. Why does that sounds familiar? Who is that?"

"He plays Nicholas Newman on *The Young and the Restless,*" John said.

"Oh, that's right. I know who he is. He's a big *SportsCenter* fan. I run into him all the time at golf events. Is he still on the show?"

"That's what we've been talking about. He's dead. Well, he's dead on the show, anyway, and we don't know if it's just a plot twist or if they killed him off because he died in real life."

"Well, let's find out." I said.

I had lost track of Josh's number, but we were doing a story that night on the Milwaukee Brewers who had just taped a segment for the *The Young and the Restless*—that's why John and Jud had been talking about the show in the first place. Over the Brewers highlight, I replaced one of my catchphrases at the time (*For the love of elevation*) with "For the love of Nick Newman."

The next day I got a message from Josh. "Linda Cohn. Long time, no talk. Josh Morrow here. I heard your shout-out on ESPN. You know I watch every day. I finally made *SportsCenter!* What a great day for me."

So Josh is not dead in real life—and it turns out he's not dead on the show either. In typical soap opera fashion, his character is alive and well, living in a cave somewhere with a full beard and a beautiful woman who's taking care of his cuts and bruises.

There's a danger though, with being exposed to all of this celebrity: Next to all my brushes with celebrity—not to mention just the everyday excitement of watching sports for a living—life at home with a marketing research consultant husband can seem kind of dull.

Imagine how a conversation in our house might go:

Me (just returning home from the Super Bowl): The Super Bowl was great, but you won't believe what happened the night before the game. I was at a pregame party and all of a sudden I found myself standing at the bar between Michael Jordan and Wayne Gretzky talking sports . . .

Me (ten minutes later): . . . and that's what happened. How did things go while I was away? What did you do?

Stew: Let's see, I sat in my office [the unadorned extra bedroom over our front door] and did an analysis of . . . [whatever Stew was doing an analysis of, it went right over my head]

Me: Oh, that's interesting. Where are the kids?

It wasn't quite as bad as all that, although I really was standing at a bar talking sports with Michael Jordan and Wayne Gretzky after the Super Bowl. And, as I would figure out later, my boredom really had nothing to do with Stew at all, or the fact that I had just been to the Super Bowl. Stew was a loving and supportive husband, and he was my rock. No matter what else was going on in my life—almost getting fired from ESPN, seeing my hopes of hosting the Hot Seat dashed, having some other emotional crisis—Stew was there to support me unconditionally and help me get through to the other side.

He was a wonderful father too. On the weekends, while I was working, he would ignore his ever-growing to-do list and instead spend time with Sam and Dan digging out snow caves, playing funny-face games, and just giving them what they needed. Every night he'd put them to bed with one of his favorite songs: "House at Pooh Corner," "Our House," "Desperado," et cetera.

One night when I was actually home, waiting for my turn to sing the kids a song of my own—my favorite was "Lights"—I overheard this conversation between Stew and my daughter after he had finished singing "Puff, the Magic Dragon" to her.

"Daddy, what ever happened to the dragon after the boy left?

"I don't know, Sammy. I heard there used to be another verse to the song, but it mysteriously vanished and no one can remember it anymore."

"I want to know what happens. The ending is too sad."

"Well, I'll see if I can find out what happened. Good night, sweetheart. I'll see you in the morning."

"Good night, Daddy."

When he came out of Sammy's room, I said, "What are you going to do now?"

He looked at me matter-of-factly and said, "I guess I'm going to write another verse to the song."

About a week later, when Stew was saying good night to Sammy, he told her, "I found out what happened to the dragon." Then he sang the song adding this verse at the end:

Deep inside his cave,
Puff's green eyes opened wide.
As he heard the sound of Sammy Jeanne,
Searching just outside.
When he rushed outside to greet her,
She smiled at who she saw.
And Puff that mighty dragon,
He commenced his fearless roar!

Like the song he had written to stop me from worrying about the kids, I didn't know if it was any good, but I think this gives you a little insight into the type of guy Stew is. Hey, he's no Wayne Gretzky, but who else is?

What I've been beating around the bush trying to say is that, unrelated to anything he was or wasn't doing, I was starting again to question whether I wanted to be married to Stew, or anyone for that matter. Internally, I'd been struggling with this for a long time. I didn't understand it, I just knew it didn't feel right and I couldn't ignore it any longer.

I sat down with Stew and told him what was on my mind. He was devastated, but we talked things over a little and agreed to go to counseling, again. Then I escaped to work and left Stew alone to ponder the future.

When I came home at three o'clock that morning, there was a poem waiting for me on the kitchen table. I cried as I read it.

Jump
I Love You

But
You are afraid to fall with me

You will not let go
of your handhold on the cliff

You have been dropped
Too many times
By those who talked of love
but acted in other ways

They cried with real, but passive tears at your pain
and told you it would be all right
Then dropped you again
Unintentionally
but with no intention at all
Then denied the cause of your pain

You deny it too
or blame it on other things
And though the bruises have healed
Your pain remains

So you are afraid to fall
But I have already taken the leap
(what am I to do now?)
I jumped when I thought you said you would come too

I know
You walked to the edge and pushed off
But as you began to fall
You reached back
Instinctively
And held to the cliff
Although it offered you nothing
but the chance to hang on
While I
Offer you the possibility
Of everything
Together

And I am left falling
Alone

Now it is up to you

You can hold tight to the cliff
With passive tears in your eyes
As you let me
crash

to

the

ground
into a pile
of
what
might have been

Or
You can jump in
and save me

But you cannot catch me
with one hand clutched to the cliff

I do not know everything
(This much I have learned)

But
I promise
If you take the leap

I will catch you
As you catch me

I will not let you drop

Jump.

I'm not much into poems. I usually don't understand them. But as I read what Stew had written to me, I understood what he was talking about and I knew he was right. Through my life I succeeded time and again by committing myself to getting what I wanted. I committed myself to getting on my high school boys' hockey team. I committed myself to succeeding as a sportscaster. I committed myself to giving my kids as much time and love as I could when I was around—anyone who visited our house could surely attest that I wasn't spending my time on housekeeping. But the truth was, I had never really committed to my marriage with Stew. I thought I loved Stew, and I said "I love you" to him frequently, but I had to admit that, emotionally, I was always holding a little bit back. I was afraid to give everything I had, because I wasn't sure it would come back to me.

We started going to counseling, and it seemed to be working. As before, just talking things through was bringing us closer together. After a few months I finally got to the point where I felt things were going well and we could handle things on our own. I was ready to stop counseling and make a commitment to Stew and our lives together.

But way down, in the darkest recesses of my mind, I knew that part of the reason I had wanted to stop going to counseling was because I was afraid. I was afraid that if we kept going to therapy, we might uncover a deeper reason for our marital problems that wasn't so easily fixed. For the moment Stew and I were both happy, and I didn't want to disturb what might be the delicate balance of our relationship.

TEN

Sex and the Female Sportscaster

Here's a little secret. Are you ready? I'm too sexy. If you didn't know, I can't blame you. It even took me some time to realize I have this awesome power that I have to keep under control.

It all started a few years ago, when they added the "Tower" segment to *SportsCenter*. This is the part of the show where one of the anchors does a story standing up in front of a screen, instead of from behind the desk. All of a sudden I had to start paying close attention to what I was wearing from the waist down, and I had to make sure I wore something different every time. You might be able to get away with wearing a nondescript blue blazer twice in two weeks, but a full outfit is more recognizable.

One day, with my wardrobe almost exhausted, I wore a skirt with opaque tights and black boots. I hardly thought it was provocative. It was a maroon-and-black-plaid wool skirt that ended just barely above the knee, plus some pretty ordinary black boots with a low heel. I hate heels and avoid them at all costs. For a top, I wore a dark, bulky sweater. It was a typical wintry outfit. I thought.

After the show, Norby called me over and said, "What's with the boots? You can't wear boots for a Tower shot. It's too distracting."

If you've ever watched me on TV, and I'm assuming you have since you're reading this book, you know that I'm very careful about wearing clothes that are appropriate for my job. I try to look attractive because it's TV, and I am a little vain, but I never wear short skirts or tight tops or anything I think is suggestive in any way—even though female sportscasters on other networks do. And it's not because I can't get away with it. I actually weigh less now than I did in college, and I'm a size 4.

In Norby's defense, he's always been kind of my resident big brother at ESPN, and I knew he was just looking out for me. Still, it seemed that over the next few months I was frequently being told I couldn't wear certain outfits because they were too tight, too revealing, or inappropriate.

I didn't see it, but maybe Norby had a point. When I met James Denton from *Desperate Housewives* at a party a year later, he said, "My friends and I watch you all the time and we play this little game where we guess what you'll be wearing when you stand in front of the big screen." I knew that was just innocent fun. And even though Shaun White, the gold-medal-winning snowboarder, only jokingly said about me, "She's awesome. I'm taking her to my prom," there were other people who seemed to be spending way too much energy paying attention to what I was wearing and giving me too much credit for the impact I had on people.

Almost exactly a year after I met Shaun at the X Games, I was back at the same X Games and checking my messages at work from my cell phone. Anyone of any importance would be calling me directly on my cell phone, so there weren't many messages. There were a few calls from admiring fans, which I always appreciated, and an absurd and raunchy call from a pair of inebriated college students who were up later than their better judgment should have allowed them. Calls like that were innocuous and always made me smile. The last call, though, was from a verbally abusive woman who accused me of corrupting her two sons. Here's a shortened, and cleaned-up, version of what she said: "You should be ashamed of yourself! What kind of message are you sending, standing there with your legs spread? My teenage boys are watching you on TV and commenting on how you look. Ladies are supposed to stand with their legs closed. You should be fired!"

No matter how long I've been around, I'm always astounded and disturbed when I come in contact with an individual whose reaction to something I've done is worse, and more mean spirited, than whatever I've done. In the situation this woman had called to berate me about, I was standing up and wearing pants. I suppose my ankles weren't locked together, but they weren't any farther apart than I needed to keep them to stop from losing my balance on the set. But the real test was that Norby never said anything about it. If Norby thought it was okay, then it was okay. But that didn't mean that the controversy around my sexuality was about to die away. The long-running ESPN commercial campaign saw to that.

As you probably know, in addition to its sports coverage, ESPN has become known for the innovative and tongue-in-cheek commercials created for it by the Wieden & Kennedy ad agency. Just real quick then, here are a couple of ESPN commercials, one of which I almost didn't make it into and the other that will never appear on TV because, well, you know, I'm just too sexy:

The ESPN Swimsuit Edition

The way Wieden & Kennedy does the ESPN commercials, or at least the way it looks to me, is that they come in for a couple of weeks with some cameramen and some creative people and develop the commercials on sight. You don't know what the commercials will be like or how many, if any, you'll be in until they pack up and leave.

During one of these two-week stints, I heard through the grapevine that Wieden & Kennedy was creating a swimsuit edition spoof. From what I heard, they had tapped a bunch of *SportsCenter* anchors to be in the commercial, but no women and, more critically, not me.

Call me crazy, but does that make sense? Who doesn't put women in a swimsuit commercial? Even if only to add a little contrast. I don't want to make any rash assumptions, but wouldn't you think the majority of ESPN viewers would rather see me in a swimsuit than Bill Pidto in his Speedo? While I have to admit Bill was hilarious in that commercial, I wasn't going to stand for it.

Casually, I went up to one of the guys from Wieden & Kennedy who was casting the commercials. I wanted to say, *What's wrong with you? Why won't you put me in the swimsuit commercial?* But instead I said, sweet as pie, "Look, I'd be happy to be in the swimsuit commercial if you want."

"Oh really? That would be great," he said, and he ended up casting me in a funny bit with Mr. Met. But in his eyes I could see he was thinking, *She's just too sexy.*

Hanging with Orlando Pace in a Hot Tub

This is a commercial you'll never see. Here's the story:

One of the people from Wieden & Kennedy approached me one day and said, "We have this idea for a 'What Really Happens at ESPN' commercial. We want to put you and Orlando Pace in a hot tub together and create the illusion that you and he are drinking champagne and partying it up in a hot tub after hours in the basement of ESPN. You're going to have to wear a bathing suit, and we wanted to make sure you were okay with it before we set it up." Of course, I said, "I'm in. Let's do it."

The day of the shoot, I'm all prepared. I head down to this little room in the basement, and there's a hot tub in there. Well, sort of. It's not so much a hot tub as it is one of those small therapeutic tubs that athletes use. Orlando is already in the water, sitting on the bench. But Orlando is 6 foot 7 and 325 pounds. The only way I can fit in the tub is if I sit on his lap. There's one guy filming the commercial and five others taking still pictures. I don't know why they need five photographers, but if ESPN says it's okay, then I'm sure it's okay.

I've never met Orlando Pace before, but I discover he's just a big sweetheart of a man. Even though we're both in bathing suits and I'm sitting on his lap in a small tub of hot, bubbling water, I don't feel uncomfortable at all. I can tell we're both thinking the same thing: *This is just one big joke, so let's have some fun with it.* It turns out pretty good, and, once the taping is done, I remember thinking that this might be the best commercial for ESPN I've ever done.

A print version of the ad ends up in the next issue of *ESPN The Magazine,* and I think it's pretty funny. I suppose, at first glance, it might cause someone to do a double take because it almost looks like I'm not wearing anything in the tub. But isn't that the point of advertising? Overall, I think the situation is so ridiculous that it can only be laughed at.

The very day the magazine comes out, I get a call from Steve Anderson. He tells me they had no idea the commercial was being shot until they saw the ad in the magazine, and they think the ad is too over the top to ever appear on the air. People might take it the wrong way. I'm listening to Steve and all I can really say is "Sure. Sure. Okay. Right. I understand. Okay. Bye." But you and I know the real truth. I'm just too sexy.

Let's talk about sexual harassment in the workplace. If you're a fan of ESPN and you've paid any attention at all to the news, you know that there have been several sexual harassment claims by women against male employees on the Bristol campus. I'd like to go on record now by saying that sexual harassment is probably the worst thing that can happen to a woman in the workplace. It puts her in a place of weakness and, no matter what the outcome, usually has a long-term negative impact on her, whether she brings it to the attention of human resources or not. As far as I'm concerned, most men who commit sexual harassment get off easy. That said, I'd also like to go on record by saying I'm not really sure what sexual harassment is. And as bad as it is, being accused of it when you're innocent is even worse.

I didn't always feel this way, but I changed my mind after a friend of mine was accused of sexual harassment and, instead of withholding judgment until I knew all the facts, I abandoned him.

Les was one of the first guys I became friendly with at ESPN. We came from similar backgrounds, and his wife reminded me of one of my favorite cousins. It was just an easy and fun friendship. We would work together on a special project now and then, but usually our jobs did not intersect. Then one day a rumor started going around the newsroom that Jennifer, a woman much younger than Les, was accusing him of sexual harassment.

I was so disturbed by the possibility that Les would have done something like this that I avoided talking to him completely. In fact, it bothered me so much that I felt obligated to reach out to Jennifer to see if I could help her get through this difficult time.

A small part of me kept thinking maybe I should get Les's side of the story, but the evidence against him seemed damning. Apparently there was a long trail of suggestive e-mails from Les to Jennifer. I felt a real empathy toward Jennifer and started helping her work through what she was going through. Les was given a three-week suspension, which seemed like little more than a slap on the wrist.

When it was all over, Jennifer and I had developed a friendship beyond the unpleasant incident that started it and we would occasionally go out together after work. That's when our relationship changed—or at least that's when I noticed the change.

Before I knew it, Jennifer was sending me five, six, or seven e-mails a day, all of them just making small talk. In my office, at the pod, even when I was on the set getting ready for a show, I would get e-mails from her. If I didn't respond to her right away, she would send me a follow-up e-mail asking if something was wrong. One night I was doing the early show and looking forward to getting home by 8:00 p.m., in time to spend some time with my kids before they went to bed. As the show was about to begin, Jennifer sent me an e-mail asking if we could go out after work.

I told her I was going to rush home right after the show so I could see my kids. Within minutes she shot back a reply, saying she thought we were friends, and she wanted to know why I was treating her this way. That's when I began to understand there was something twisted about the way Jennifer looked at the world. I started distancing myself from her, enduring a battery of barbed e-mails from her for a couple of weeks until she finally let me go and then, most likely, latched on to someone else. It was then I was able to see things from Les's point of view.

After a while I finally got up the courage to approach Les and talk to him about what had happened. He told me that when Jennifer started working at ESPN, the two of them had struck up what he thought of as an innocently flirtatious friendship. It started with an in-person banter between them that overflowed into e-mails. Jennifer was almost fifteen years younger than Les, who was happily married with two kids. In his own mind, there was never anything more going on than a couple of coworkers who were working in close quarters and, under intense pressure, letting off a little steam.

Then, just as in my relationship with Jennifer, she started demanding more time and attention from Les. When Les started thinking things were becoming inappropriate and tried to get them in check, Jennifer went off the deep end. Based on my own experience with her, Les's side of the story rung true, but he was punished just the same. The three-week suspension was the least of it. The most difficult part was going to work every day with a tarnished image and trying to make his wife understand and believe his story.

In my own experience, there was an incident a few years ago when a longtime and close colleague of mine (you wouldn't know who he was even if I mentioned his name) started interacting with me in a way I thought was inappropriate. Do you want to know what I did? I took him aside one day and, in private, told him his behavior was making me feel uncomfortable. You know what he did? He apologized and told me he hadn't even realized that he was making me uncomfortable, and it never happened again. Today we're as close and comfortable with each other as we ever were. It's amazing what a little open communication can do.

Since I'm exhausting the subject of sex in this chapter, I'd like to talk a little bit about the combination of women, sports, and sex. By the time you read this book, the hoopla will probably have died down, but as I was writing it, there were a lot of news stories about Amanda Beard that got me thinking. The issue at hand isn't about Amanda Beard, per se, but she does bring to light something that's been on my mind for a long time.

If you're a fan of Olympic swimming, you probably know Amanda because she's a three-time Olympic medalist (1996, 2000, 2004); she won her first gold medal at fourteen while carrying her 3-foot-tall teddy bear around the Olympic Village. If you're not a fan of the sport, then you've probably heard of her because, in 2007, she appeared nude in an eight-page spread in *Playboy*.

I'm not criticizing her appearance in *Playboy*, because I don't really know how I feel. There's something about it that disturbs me, and something else that makes me think it's no big deal. In the interest of full disclosure, when I was in my late twenties, I wanted to appear in *Playboy* myself, even though no one was asking. While working day and night to establish my credentials as a legitimate sportscaster, I was thinking, *Wouldn't it be cool to appear in* Playboy? Now I'm glad I didn't, although it would have been a rush. Can you imagine?

So I don't begrudge Amanda's decision, but part of me is trying to figure out why. There's all this talk about appreciating an athletic female body and being a role model for young girls. I've seen the pictures, and it's true that Amanda does have a fine athletically toned body. But the pictures are clearly not a celebration of athleticism; they're sensual to say the least, not that there's anything wrong with that. Let's be honest, though: We all know why men of all ages look at *Playboy*, and it doesn't have anything to do with appreciating the athletic female body, at least not the way it's been put out there.

And what of being a role model for young women? What do we say to our twelve-year-old daughters when a woman who has spent many years working long and hard to achieve success in her chosen field takes her clothes off for *Playboy*? Are we saying that appearing in *Playboy* is the ultimate achievement for every woman regardless of what else she's done? Are we saying it's okay to use sex to sell ourselves and increase our marketability?

Isn't what it really boils down to when we applaud behavior like this—we're saying to children and adults alike that it's okay to do whatever it takes to be popular? Is that wrong?

It's something I've wrestled with most of my career. Why isn't it enough for me to just be good at my job? Why do I have to (and want to) try to look as attractive as I possibly can on the air? Why do I always have the feeling that when my looks finally go, then so will my career? Why did I feel it was necessary for me to mention at the beginning of this chapter that I'm a size 4? Does that make me better at my job? Does it make me a better person? These are questions I ask myself all the time, and I'm no closer to having answers for them now than I was when I first posed them. That's what really bothers me.

ELEVEN

As Scripted?
Not So Much

L ife is filled with losses and gains. Don't you think? My mother always told me I could do anything I wanted if I put my mind to it. I still believe that's true. In fact, I've pretty much built my career on that belief. But what I've come to realize is that sometimes you get less than you need and sometimes you get more, regardless of how hard you try.

There was a time for me a few years ago when I was becoming interested in hip-hop and R&B, and I knew a lot of NBA players listened to hip-hop to get motivated before a game. I also knew Jay-Z was a big NBA fan—and that NBA star Tracy McGrady was a big Jay-Z fan. Just before the All-Star Game in Philly, I got the idea that maybe I could get the two of them to do an interview together. I called the PR department at the Orlando Magic and they said that of course Tracy would be interested in talking to Jay-Z. Then I called Jay-Z's "people," who told me he would definitely be interested in meeting with Tracy, as long as I could guarantee the interview would be a "Sunday Conversation" piece and that it would be aired multiple times (which was the policy at ESPN anyway). Jay-Z was in New York and he was going to have to travel out to Philly to do the interview, so he wanted to make sure it was going to be worth his effort. I checked with programming at ESPN just to make sure; they said they could guarantee the piece would air at least eight times. That was good enough for Jay-Z.

I remember how happy I was that I was going to be able to bring two big stars together to talk about two of their favorite things, sports and music. Monday morning I flew out to Philadelphia—and it was great. The two of them just bounced off each other as if they were long-lost friends.

Back at the studio, Jason Sobel, my editor, came up to me and said, "Linda, you know what we can do? We can intercut the interview with Jay-Z music videos."

"Brilliant!" I said, and he put together this unbelievable piece.

Sunday morning, I'm home watching the "Sunday Conversation" and I'm very happy with how it all turned out. I'm just sitting in front of the TV, beaming. I'm so proud that I put this idea together and that I was able to make it happen. I'm beginning to think the piece is so good that they'll run it all week. Jay-Z and Tracy will be so happy.

Then the phone rings. It's Norby. He says, "I appreciate the effort you made on that McGrady–Jay-Z piece, but it's not running, ever again."

"What do you mean?" I say. "Don't you think it's a good piece?"

"It has to do with the music and the videos. We don't have permission to use them."

Apparently, even though Jason thought we were cleared to use the music, we weren't. It didn't matter that we were using Jay-Z's music and Jay-Z was in the piece. It had to go through legal channels, and that just wasn't going to happen in time. If we continued to run the piece, Norby told me, it could have cost ESPN hundreds of thousands of dollars in fees.

Losing the piece was bad enough, but then I had to call up Jay-Z's manager to tell him I wasn't going to be able to keep my promise. The piece had aired once and it wasn't going to air ever again. He seemed to understand, but I never spoke to Jay-Z or his people after that.

Do you want to hear how I almost lost my unofficial lifetime membership as a Mets fan? It was May 2004, and the team had just lost its fourth game in a row. It was early in the season, but it looked like it was going to be a tough year for my beloved Mets. I was doing research for the highlight, and I saw that things were going to get worse before they got better. The next team they were playing was the red-hot Astros, whose best pitchers were coming up in the rotation. On the air, I was commiserating with the Mets, because it looked like they were going to have to wait until the Astros series was over before they would be able to get out of their slump. During the highlight, I said, "The Mets are 0 and 4 in their last four games and it doesn't get any better because they have to face the Houston Astros and the pitching rotation of Roger Clemens, Andy Pettitte, and Roy Oswalt. Can you say 0 and 7?"

A couple of days later, I received flowers from the Mets organization. The card said, "Linda, thanks for all your support. Your friends at the Mets." It's no secret to the Mets organization that I'm a die-hard Mets fan, and I thought to myself, *This is great. They really understand how much I care about them, and how much I sympathize about their situation.* I was really thrilled that the Mets had sent me flowers, and I was telling everyone in the studio who would listen.

I was working with Steve Berthiaume that night, and all through the show he was making obtuse flower references, interjecting things into the broadcast like, "You don't bring me flowers," and "That deserves a bouquet of flowers." The next day I saw Peter Gammons, our baseball guru; still giddy from receiving the flowers, I couldn't wait to tell Peter all about it.

When I was done, he said, "Yeah I heard about that."

I said, "You did? Did you talk to the Mets? Who should I talk to? Who should I thank?"

"Well, actually, Linda, there was something you said over a highlight that they didn't think was very funny. They didn't send you the flowers as a thank-you. It was meant to be sarcastic. They thought you were ripping them. They're all pretty mad at you: Jay Horowitz, John Franco, Todd Zeile, and Mike Piazza."

I was crushed. "Are you kidding? I love the Mets. I wasn't making fun of them. I was commiserating with them. Now I don't know what I'm going to do."

Harold Reynolds had heard my whole conversation with Peter and he said, "Hey, Linda, I have Todd's phone number if you want to call him."

So I called Todd Zeile to apologize. "I love you guys. I would never put you guys down. You have to forgive me. I was just looking at the tough road you were going to have with the Astros and I was commiserating with you."

But Todd's a real jokester. He kept saying things like, "I don't know, Linda. The guys are pretty mad at you. I don't think an apology is going to cut it for what you said about us on the air . . . ," just to hear me beg some more, until I finally realized he was playing with me, and he let me off the hook.

But after that, the Mets went on a winning streak, so I can only think my remarks on the air spurred them on and that I really did deserve those flowers. I'll tell you one thing. If I'm ever in a situation like that again, I won't hesitate to get the Mets mad at me if it means I might be able to pull them out of their slump.

As it turned out, I wouldn't be in a position to do that for a while, because it would be some time before I worked *Sports-Center* again on a regular basis during baseball season. You know how they say, be careful what you wish for because it just might come true? Well, it did for me.

When Norby first offered me a regular slot on the 1:00 a.m. *SportsCenter* shift, he warned me that I probably wouldn't be able to cope with the arduous schedule for more than a couple of years. No one else had, but six or seven years later, I was still the mainstay on that show.

While I loved doing *SportsCenter,* I wanted to do other things as well. ESPN would let me off the *SportsCenter* set once in a while to do the NFL draft, the X Games, or some interviews, but I always wanted something more permanent. All my colleagues, or so it seemed to me, were associated with a major sport or show other than *SportsCenter,* and that's what I wanted as well.

Periodically I would approach ESPN with a request like "Let me host a hockey show" or "I'd like to have a regular gig with the NFL." ESPN Radio had also expressed interest in having me do a daily show, and I asked about that. But no matter what I came to management with, even if I had support from a show's producer, my request was always met with the same response: "You're too valuable on *SportsCenter* for us to let you do anything else on a regular basis."

Then, in the spring of 2005, ESPN approached me with a new contract and said, basically, "You've been telling us for years that you want to branch out and do other things. Well, we've been listening We're going to take you completely off *SportsCenter* and assign you to do WNBA play-by-play, some PGA coverage, the *NFL Blitz,* and some other things that we're still working on."

Whoa! All this other stuff was great, but I never said I wanted to be kicked off *SportsCenter.* It was like losing an old friend. I'd been identified with that show forever. But it was too late. I was told they were completely reformulating the show and that I couldn't do both *SportsCenter* and these other things.

Well, okay. It wasn't exactly what I had in mind, but it was my job, so I did it. The WNBA turned out to be pretty cool, although it took a lot of work at first. Since it was one of the few athletic organizations with which I was almost completely unfamiliar, I had to learn the rules (they're different from those of the NBA), learn all the players, and learn how to do play-by-play before the season started. It helped that the broadcast crew smoothed my transaction by welcoming me with open arms. And the WNBA itself is a wonderful organization from the top down, with players and coaches who are in the WNBA for only one reason: They love the game.

Lucky for me, not every one of my new assignments was as unfamiliar to me as the WNBA. Golf is one of my favorite sports to play and watch, so covering PGA tournaments was a gift as far as I'm concerned. But by far the best thing that came out of my switch away from *SportsCenter* was my chance to host the *NFL Blitz,* only partly because I love football. Doesn't everybody?

The *NFL Blitz* is completely different from anything else I've ever done. Unlike other shows, where everything is mapped out on a rundown sheet, the *Blitz* is almost completely spontaneous and gives us more license to be just a little bit more opinionated. Often the show starts before any of the games for the day are even done, so Mike Hill, Qadry Ismail, and I just pick a topic and start talking. Once the games end, the chaos begins.

I might start with, say, a Colts–Patriots highlight. I get a shot sheet thrown in front of me telling what I'll be seeing in the highlight, but the last shot is missing because they had to rush the sheet in so that I could start the highlight. While I'm doing the highlight, I've got the producer, Jeff Ross, in my ear telling me what story or highlight I'll be throwing to when I'm done. At the same time, I'm alternating my attention between the highlight I'm doing and the Giants–Eagles game on the screen next to me. In the Giants game, Jay Feely is lining up to kick the game-winning field goal. I can't miss that. Meanwhile, I'm reading off the last shot on my shot sheet and waiting for Jeff to come back in my ear and give me the "crossover" before I run out of shot sheet. As always, there he is in my ear just in time. At this point, I'm flying blind, just repeating exactly what Jeff's saying: "Peyton Manning . . . 40-yard touchdown pass . . . to Marvin Harrison." As I'm saying this, I see the Giants miss their field goal, so I just add, conversationally, "Can you believe Jay

Feely just missed the game-winning field goal? That can't happen. We'll get back to that later. Right now . . . ," and I throw it over to Mike.

While Mike is doing his highlight, Jeff tells me I'll be doing a Q&A with one of our reporters, either Sal Paolantonio or Ed Werder. This can be the most challenging part of the show, because I haven't spent the last three hours watching whatever game we'll be talking about. Still, I can't just say, "What's happening Ed?" or "That was some game, huh, Sal?" I have to really know what's going on so I can ask an intelligent question.

While we're talking about intelligent questions, let me tell you that I really hate when people in my business conduct an entire interview without asking a single question. You know what I mean. These are the people who start off every interview with, "Hey Joe Athlete, great game! Tell me what was going through your head today." Or they ask a question that's so biased that you already know the answer before the athlete opens his mouth: "There must have been a lot of pressure on you today. How did you feel?" No matter how the athlete was feeling— challenged, relaxed, pumped up, scared, or angry—at this point he's going to say, "Well, I guess I was feeling pressured."

Don't say to me, "Oh Linda, that's how everybody does interviews these days. It's just the style." It's not the style, and if you don't believe me, go watch an interview with Andrea Kramer, Jeremy Schapp, or Pam Oliver. Instead of reaching for the remote, or letting your mind wander over to what's in the fridge, you might feel compelled to actually listen to the interview.

Getting back to golf, a long time ago, before we had even moved to Seattle, I bought Stew a set of golf clubs to celebrate his earning his MBA. I figured if he was going to be entering the world of upper management, he was going to have to learn how to play golf. Naturally, I bought myself a set of clubs as well, even though neither one of us really knew how to play. Since we lived and worked pretty far from anything that resembled a golf course, we took our first lessons inside a Baruch College gym on Twenty-sixth Street, practicing with those little waffle golf balls.

Over the years I grew to become a fairly decent golfer, and by the time I'd been working at ESPN for a few years, I was getting invited to celebrity golf tournaments on a regular basis. Once the word got around that I could actually play, it wasn't long until I was invited to a Celebrity Players Tournament. The difference between the types of events I usually played in and a Celebrity Players Tournament was that the former is usually done for charity, while in a Celebrity Players Tournament you actually get paid to play.

As the date for the tournament was getting closer, I started fantasizing that I might be able to start a second career on the celebrity players tour with people like Gary Carter, Rick Rhoden, and Mark Rypien. I had been playing almost every week, and there were always a shortage of women on these tours. I thought I had a real chance.

As luck would have it, for this tournament, I was teamed up with Gary Carter, the Mets legend! It was really exciting for me to be playing with one of the greatest Mets of all time. Gary was wonderful, but, as you're probably expecting by now, when I played in the tournament it was a disaster. On the first day I hit a 135 and came in dead last. On the sixteenth hole I four-putted from 10 feet away. I was throwing off the whole rhythm of our team. Gary went from being happy to meet and play with me to wishing he had never ever heard of me. On the second day they had to reseed me to avoid affecting the other players. My confidence was completely shot.

But that's not the end of the story. A few weeks later I was playing in the Jimmy V Celebrity Golf Classic, which raises valuable money for cancer research. Coming off the Pro-Am, I had lost all my confidence and couldn't hit anything right. In these charity events you always play in a foursome, and you usually play "best ball," so even if you're stinking things up, it doesn't really matter. You just pick up your ball, move it to wherever the best player in your foursome has hit, and continue from there.

Well, I got through the eighteen holes and I don't think my shot was the "best ball" more than twice. I wasn't feeling too good about my golf capabilities at the time, but after the tournament, they had a "closest to the pin" contest, just for fun. I'm always up for a challenge and I wasn't going to let my bad day on the course ruin my chance to get closest to the pin, so I entered the contest.

It was a par-three, 160-yard hole and, while I waited for my turn, I was trying to figure out which club to use. One hundred sixty yards isn't that far, and everyone else was using irons. I hit a pretty good drive, but since I wasn't feeling that confident, I pulled out my 7-wood to be on the safe side. The fairway was lined with people watching; I didn't want to totally embarrass myself for the day by coming up short on a 160-yard drive.

When it was my turn, I placed my ball on the tee, took a couple of practice swings, and then hauled off as hard as I could.

It was a lousy shot. I shanked it to the left and, like a bullet, it went right into the crowd. I didn't get any lift on the ball at all, so there wasn't time for anyone to move. I hit a sixteen-year-old kid right in the side of the head, and he slumped to the ground. It was so horrifying and unexpected that there was an audible gasp from the crowd.

I ran over to see if the kid was okay. They examined him for a few minutes and then took him away. *Thank God I didn't kill him,* I thought. Rich Eisen and Stuart Scott were hosting the tournament, and they tried to make me feel better. They were telling me it wasn't my fault and that things like this happened, but I knew it was my fault. I had no business competing in that contest based on the way I had been playing.

Later that day, as I was trying to forget the whole thing with copious amounts of food from the buffet table, someone tapped me on the shoulder. It was that same young man, and he had the golf ball I'd hit him with in his hand. He was smiling, so I knew he wasn't coming over to tell me his parents were going to sue me for everything I had. He said, "Hi, Linda. I'm the guy you hit with the golf ball. Would you sign it for me?"

I signed the ball and apologized to him over and over again, and that was the end of that. He hadn't really been hurt at all, but I was still shaken. I knew if the ball had hit him in a different spot on his head, the outcome could have been very different. I didn't pick up a club again for a whole year. I thought, What if it had been one of my kids out there?

Speaking of my kids, one of the advantages of being a semi-celebrity is that you get to share your perks with them. For instance, we had been to Disney so often by the time my daughter was eight years old that she freely shared with anyone who asked her about her most recent trip that she definitely preferred Disneyland to Disney World. And when the four of us go somewhere as a family, it's not unusual for someone to say to either Sam or Dan, "It must be great to have Linda Cohn as your mother."

The truth, though, is that while they're aware that some other people are impressed by what I do, it hardly matters to them. When Sammy was twelve, she took it all in stride when one of her guy friends invited her to an end-of-the-school-year pool party and added, "Maybe your mom can come too." Likewise, when Dan was younger, he couldn't understand why an attractive man he had never seen came up to me at a Mets game and spoke to me for fifteen minutes. "Is that your boyfriend?" he asked.

Both of my children enjoy playing and watching sports. Sammy, who is now sixteen, plays on her high school tennis team and, to my delight, has become a serious Rangers fan. After trying almost every sport there is, Dan now plays lacrosse and basketball and, at eleven years old, has chosen to torture me by becoming a Yankees fan. But they are hardly fanatics, and don't live and die by the outcome of each game, so I am often overruled when I try to switch the television from SpongeBob or a reality show to watch a midseason game. "Why are you always watching sports?" is not an uncommon refrain in our home, and my response—"Um, because it's my job"—doesn't usually cut it.

Recently, after the Rangers signed both Scott Gomez and Chris Drury during the free-agent signing period, and after I screamed in ecstasy, I was explaining it to Dan and said, "I can't believe we signed both Gomez and Drury." Dan and I were in the kitchen together and he looked up from his cookies and milk and asked, "What do you mean, 'we'?" It looks like Dan will never be a Rangers fan. Oh well, I guess we all have our little disappointments.

Here was another one. In late 2004 I was once again feeling unhappy with my marriage to Stew. Actually, I was feeling miserable. Even though I didn't quite understand why, I would often cry when I thought about my marriage or, sometimes, for no particular reason at all.

To everyone we knew, it probably looked like Stew was the perfect fit for me. He was supportive of me in every way, was never jealous of my success, gave me whatever freedom (within reason) I needed, loved the children as much as I did, and had made major sacrifices in his own career and lifestyle so that I could pursue my career goals.

When I sat down with Stew and told him, once again, that I was thinking of ending our marriage, I could see that this cycle I was putting him through was really starting to take its toll on him. This time, when we started seeing a new therapist, she asked us what we wanted to get out of this therapy. I told her I just wanted to understand why I felt this way. Stew said he didn't want to be "here" ever again, meaning that he was tired of riding the roller coaster I had kept him on over the last twenty years that always ended up putting him back in the same spot.

From the very start, we knew this therapy was going to take us somewhere we hadn't been before. In our past experiences with counseling, we'd almost always come out of a session feeling uplifted and optimistic. With our new therapist, we always left feeling like crap.

Early on in our sessions, the therapist explored the possibility that I might be clinically depressed and suggested I consider going on a Prozac-like drug to see if that made me feel any better. As you might expect, I was totally against it. I was sad a lot of the time, but I never felt hopeless or as if my life wasn't worth living. I loved life. I was also afraid taking something like that would change my personality and, you know what, I really liked myself quite a bit. That was another sign that I wasn't actually depressed. We abandoned that course of action and plodded forward, looking for other answers.

Over the period of a few months, the therapist helped me understand that the problems I was having in my marriage were due, in part, to me being a thrill junkie. Excitement was my drug, and I was addicted. It's a very complicated issue, and I'm not going to take you through a whole year of therapy, but basically what I learned was that starting at a very early age, I used the excitement of sports to combat my loneliness and lack of friends. Later, when I became more confident and developed meaningful friendships, I need more to get "high" and stepped up my addiction by tapping into the excitement and adulation of my broadcasting career.

A second factor coming into play was that I'd grown up in a household perpetually filled with drama. Either my mother was yelling and screaming and generally creating tumult, or we were celebrating something. We would celebrate anything, no matter how big or small. A Giants win was cause for a major party and self-congratulation, but a minor everyday success, like getting a B on a test or winning a friendly game of tennis against a middle-aged woman at The Club, created the same level of excitement. That's the environment I had grown up in and I had adapted to it. I was comfortable with the highs and lows, but not the middle.

Stew, on the other hand, was more laid back and easygoing than anyone else I had ever met. That's probably one of the things that attracted me to him in the first place. The only problem was that in comparison with all of the highs and lows I was experiencing everywhere else in my life, Stew was like the eye of the storm. Some women might have treasured the sanctuary he provided, but for me it was like a crash into oblivion. Nothing was happening! It was suffocating.

The therapist said that if the marriage was going to survive, I would have to learn to be okay with living in the eye of the storm sometimes. She also said we needed to spend more time by ourselves, nurturing our relationship. I had visited New Orleans a few years earlier for a story I was doing on the Saints, and ever since I'd wanted to take Stew there. It had all the things he liked: drinking beer in the street, fresh oysters, and live music everywhere, to name a few.

We were both really excited about the idea, and the first night we were in New Orleans was perfect. We were both relaxed, took in the scene, drank beer on the street, and met lots of fun-loving people. The next day we were down in the French Quarter, walking by the fortune-tellers, when I was persuaded by one of them to have my fortune told. I sent Stew to an open-air bar nearby and spent the next hour with this woman.

She must have picked up on the turmoil in my head, because she drew out all my emotional demons. By the time we were done, the last thing I wanted to do was spend time with Stew, but I couldn't just tell him that a fortune-teller had made me rethink everything in my life. I knew she couldn't really tell the future, but a lot of what she had said seemed to make sense just the same. I tried to make believe everything was all right, but I couldn't. Instead of being a time for us to refresh our relationship, it was probably the worst weekend we'd had together since we moved to Seattle.

Over the next several months, we continued to go to therapy, and things were not going well. I was learning more and more about myself—and most of what I was learning was pointing me in a direction away from Stew—but I kept resisting. I knew a lot of what I had with Stew was really good, and I was afraid I might be throwing away the best thing that ever happened to me, and my best friend.

Eventually I realized I wasn't going to be able to figure this all out unless Stew and I separated. I had never lived anywhere other than with my parents or Stew, and I had no perspective on what life would be without him. One afternoon, when the kids were in school, I sat down with Stew and, through tears, explained to him that I needed a trial separation. Stew understood and he said, "It's funny somehow. You're leaving me, but after all we've gone through recently I feel closer to you now than ever before."

Since Stew was the primary caregiver, it made sense for me to look for a place nearby to live. I was taking my time looking because neither one of us could bear the thought of telling the kids what was going on. Both Dan and Sam had friends whose parents had been through divorces and they had each told us, without any prompting from us, "Don't ever get divorced."

We tried to put up a good front for the kids, but Stew and I were each living under our own little clouds of sadness. I knew living with Stew wasn't working, but I wasn't sure leaving was the right decision. At home, we were cordial to each other, but any optimism had drained from both of our hearts. Then, as corny as it sounds, I was listening to the radio and heard Keith Urban's "You'll Think of Me" for the first time. It was a story of a woman who left her man for what she thought was a better life and then regretted it, while the man went on with his life and got over her. It seemed almost exactly what was going to happen if I left Stew. At dinner I casually asked him, "Did you hear that new song, "You'll Think of Me?"

He looked up and said, "Yeah." Then he went back to his plate. I could tell he was identifying with the song too, but what else was there for him to say? Through the ups and down of our marriage, he had pretty much said everything he could. I had made the decision to leave and it was all up to me. After that night, I started thinking about everything we had been through: the laughs and tears, crises with the kids, his gentle guidance and love, and everything else that goes along with twenty years of marriage—and I realized I wasn't ready to let all that go. But by now our relationship was a shredded mess. We hardly spoke to each other, and Stew was like a guy on death row who had used up all his appeals. He knew the end was near and there was nothing left for him to do but wait for the inevitable. No matter how crazy it seemed, I had to change that. Everything that seemed right just a few weeks before now just seemed all wrong.

"I don't want to move out," I said one day when the kids were away. "You're right. I've never really committed myself to our marriage and I'm ready to do that. I don't know if I can fix what's wrong, but I'm willing to try. What do you think?"

Stew hesitated as if he wasn't sure of what he was hearing. "I think," he said, "we have so much together it would be crazy for us not to try one more time."

And that's what we did. The following December we took our annual drive out to Cleveland to visit with Stew's brother, Bob, and his family. Stew and I stayed at the Holiday Inn nearby, while the kids stayed at the house.

Although we hadn't planned it, those few nights at the Holiday Inn turned out to be among the best times we'd had in a long while. They weren't anything special. It was just the two of us, every night, by ourselves, watching movies and drinking champagne from cheap plastic glasses, not worrying about anything other than ourselves. Maybe I was learning to live in the eye of the storm, at least some of the time.

When I first started writing this book, this is where I thought it would end. But just about a month before the last segment was due on my publisher's desk, I was lying upstairs in my bedroom, watching the Mets game. During the bottom of the seventh inning, Stew came upstairs and started watching with me. The Mets were not doing too well and we watched the game in relative silence until I went into the bathroom and started crying, quietly, so Stew wouldn't hear me.

After a few minutes Stew came in. When he saw I was crying, he asked me, sympathetically, what was wrong. I said, "I want a separation."

The truth is, for the last six months I had been very unhappy and was back to seeing our therapist. At first, I thought it really had nothing to do with my marriage, but, over time, I realized my marriage to Stew was integral to everything in my life, including these feelings of unhappiness I had been having. We had been married for twenty-two years and I shared everything with him, but now, when I looked at him, I felt nothing. Sure, I appreciated Stew, and I liked him and even still cared about him, but I didn't feel anything that even slightly resembled what a wife should feel for her husband.

The therapist asked me how I would feel if Stew and I split up and I saw him with another woman. I told her, in all honesty, that I would be happy. That wasn't one of the answers she'd expected, but it made perfect sense to me. I wanted Stew to be happy, but I didn't want to have to be the one to make him happy. Stew deserved better than me.

On August 17, 2007, after 22 years of marriage and 28 years of being a couple, I slept in the house we'd shared for the last time. I don't know what's going to happen, but I do know that I've made the right decision because I felt a tremendous sense of relief when I finally moved out, even if I, someone who once had no friends at all, was now leaving the best friend I'd ever had.

So there it is. Not exactly the storybook ending I was hoping for, but the truth. I've always taken pride in being able to juggle a successful career, a happy marriage, and the raising of two children. I can't say that anymore. Still, I guess my mother was right: You can have anything you want if you put your mind to it. But what she didn't tell me was that you can't have *everything* you want. Life is full of compromises and, probably for the better, I've made mine.

As I write this, the kids have just gone back to school. Sammy is in her junior year of high school, class president, playing on the tennis team, writing for the school newspaper, and just about ready to take her driving test. Dan has just begun middle school and is busy with lacrosse, basketball, and Scouts. Now that the kids are a little older and need him less, Stew is restructuring his business to enable him to do more of what he really wants with it. His face doesn't light up anymore when he looks at me, but he says he's going to be okay, and I know he will be. Stew is one of those of people who will always end up okay. And when Stew says he's okay, he's doing better than many people are when they say they're doing "great."

As for me, I think the future is bright and I'm looking forward to living it. I've made my bed and I'm ready to lie in it. All any of us can hope for is to make the best decisions we're capable of making at any given time. That's what I've done. As I write this, it's springtime and, for me, that means the Stanley Cup playoffs and the start of baseball. When you're a sports fan, the new season always brings new possibilities.

Epilogue

Now that we've come to the end of this book, I find myself beginning to wonder what kind of impact I might end up making on this world. I have no illusions of grandeur. I never consciously set out to be a role model for other women, or men, who are out there trying to follow a dream that didn't make sense to the outside world. I just followed my own dream. I don't expect that in a hundred years my bio will still be on Wikipedia, if Wikipedia even still exists. Nothing is permanent, but we all touch so many people in our lives that we end up having an impact on the world, whether we want to or not, and often in ways we may never know of or have intended. Sometimes I think it would be nice to know that, overall, I had made a positive impact. If for no other reason than it's better than making a negative one.

Last year I picked up a goalie stick for the first time in many years to play deck hockey (rubber floored rink and sneakers). To honor tradition, I played for a women's team and a men's team. By the time the season was over, I knew I had to lace up my skates again and get back out on the ice. There's a great hockey store not too far from where I live, and they have a separate room downstairs just for goalie equipment. As I was trying on different pieces of gear, I saw something I never thought I'd live to see: a pair of kids' goalie pads in *pink*. I smiled. When I was in high school, I was the first girl in the area anyone had ever seen playing ice hockey. Now there were enough girls playing that they were making goalie equipment just for them. I know *I* wasn't the reason they were making goalie pads in pink, but maybe my playing ice hockey, in a time and place where it seemed crazy for a girl to do something like that, in some way contributed to the greater force that led to the existence of pink goalie pads. If that's true, then maybe I can believe that I've had some net positive effect on the universe. And if that's true, maybe that's enough.

This, now, is really all I have to say. At least for the time being. If you've made it this far with me, I thank you, and I wish for you what I wish for myself:

May you always be able to put yourself in a position to be lucky and, every once in a while, may the ice melt for you all on its own.

Index

About the Author

Linda Cohn is a longtime anchor of ESPN's *SportsCenter* and currently cohosts the live weekday 6:00–9:00 a.m. EST edition. She has filled a myriad of roles including hosting ESPNEWS's *NFL Blitz* and ESPN2's *College Football Saturdays*. She made history in 1987 by becoming the first full-time U.S. female sports anchor on a national radio network, when hired by ABC. Her TV career began in 1988. Cohn lives in Southbury, Connecticut.